...llo here
...oon was
...fied of a
...ea hole

...lit a fire in the fireplace in the ...
...aught here red on
...was more I
...I don't ... Sorry horrible. Very Brown
...the ferry ...
...single beds. smaller than a train. I was
...in shoce. The rooms ...

We
... Au
...s. Au
... wr...

JOYRIDE

ORO Editions

JOYRIDE

An Architect's Journey to Mexico's
Ancient and Colonial Places

DAVID C. MARTIN with **Stephanie Woodard**

This is not what happened in Mexico

but what I remembered later as my journal of the trip came together.

CONTENTS

SPARK OF
AN IDEA

When I was an undergraduate studying architecture at the University of Southern California, architectural joyrides were a Friday-night tradition. We students had been working hard all week and needed a break, though not from our favorite subject. We would pile into a Volkswagen bug and zip around Los Angeles. We might go to Bunker Hill, where we wanted to get a look at Victorian houses that we'd heard were about to be torn down. Or we would zoom over to Union Station, which, at the time, was not often used. Few people traveled by train in those days, and it was like a ghost town in the middle of the city. I am not sure how we managed it without being caught, but we piloted our VW through waiting rooms, down corridors, and along train tunnels.

Over the course of these jaunts, I immersed myself in the spatial, textural, and social elements of all kinds of architecture. They were incredible, visceral experiences of many types of built spaces. Later, while obtaining my graduate degree at Columbia University in New York City, I received a travel fellowship that allowed me to travel the world and observe great public spaces such as Piazza San Marco in Venice, Marrakesh's Jemaael-Fnaa, and the Golden Temple in Amritsar, India.

Years later, I embarked on the architectural adventure I describe in these pages. It was just as thrilling as those undergraduate escapades and also involved a vehicle, though it was certainly more carefully planned. Over the course of this journey, I sought to deepen my understanding of Mexico's architecture, from the out-of-the-way mission churches of Baja California to the graceful colonial cities and imposing ancient sites.

02

01 (previous page)
Crossing the Sea of Cortés below Cabo San Lucas.

02
This car, seen in 1973 on the plaza at Misión San Francisco Javier de Viggé-Biaundó, was the beginning of my first true race car.

03
I'm at the helm of the *Sumatra II* during an offshore race in the early 1970s.

I had nurtured a spark of this idea since my college days, when architectural history professor, Carleton Winslow Jr., told us about a month he had just spent in Mexico. He showed us a color photograph of the eighteenth-century church of Misión San Francisco Javier de Viggé-Biaundó, near a tiny, nearly inaccessible Baja California village—thirty miles straight up into the mountains from the nearest large town. Neither I, nor anyone I knew, was aware of architecture of such significance in Baja, let alone any that old or remote. At the time, there were no paved roads anywhere near the site of the mission.

Also curious to me, the mission had originally been a Jesuit institution. My parochial-school education had taught me that Padre Junípero Serra, founder of the California mission system with which I was most familiar, was a Franciscan. No one had ever mentioned the Jesuits. Over the next forty years, these intriguing notions drove me to visit half of Baja's eighteen Jesuit mission sites—eight of which have stone churches, with the remainder in ruins, including adobe churches and other buildings that have melted away to one degree or another over the centuries. I traveled by way of motorcycle, dune buggy, and jeep.

A few years ago, there was a second spark—in truth, more like a bolt of lightning. I heard about a lost mission deep in the canyons of northern Mexico. Not only was it lost, it was supposedly the last Jesuit mission founded in the New World. That was it. I had to go to Mexico and find it.

The opportunity to do so soon arose. I had helped AC Martin—the Los Angeles–based family firm where I have long been design principal—secure three major architectural commissions. However, work would not be under way for several months, and I knew that down-time between projects is an opportunity to explore and expand your vision of your profession. It is valuable time, a chance to step out of the work environment—to take a sabbatical, so to speak.

With an itinerary including Baja and Mexico's mainland—where, among other efforts, I would seek out the mysterious Jesuit mission—this learning opportunity promised much. As an architect, I am interested in the physical forms left by both contemporary and ancient societies. In discerning how and why the forms were constructed; we can find the successful architectural strategies and adapt them for our own use. Since seeing the Mexican sacred places I describe in the upcoming pages, I have completed commissions for churches and chapels and, in designing them, have found myself thinking about the ways those sites created spaces for ritual. Sometimes, when I examined an unfamiliar structure, or a collection of them, these useful aspects came to the fore; sometimes it was the site's purely sculptural characteristics that moved my soul.

The roads on my intended path through Mexico would be rough, even if some had been improved throughout the decades I had been visiting there. I decided that a jeep with a long wheelbase would handle pitted, rocky tracks and still provide a comfortable ride. Family members would come along for parts of the trip, so the vehicle had to accommodate several people. Things happened quickly. In a matter of weeks, I secured the vehicle and necessary travel papers and had a schedule for the comings and goings of family. From the U.S. State Department, I learned which roads and even entire cities to avoid because of the ongoing drug war and potential danger. I continued doing pre-trip research on the sites.

I discovered the legendary Jesuit Mission I was keen on observing, just in the nick of time before I began my excursion. I even saw it mentioned briefly in a New York Times travel article about Mexico's rugged and scenic Copper canyon—deeper than our Grand Canyon and a popular tourist destination. According to the Times, La Misión de Santo Ángel Custodio de Satevó was in the northern Mexico state of Chihuahua. My further reading revealed that the Society of Jesus founded the mission in 1699 to convert and minister to the area's Tarahumara Indians. This was just about the time the religious order was beginning its work in Baja. The existing stone church, Iglesias San Miguel de Satevó, was finished in 1764. This was toward the end of the Jesuit period in Mexico, but it was not the order's very last church.

So why all the mystery? It turned out that in the late 1800s, a fire roared through the mission, destroying buildings and records but sparing the church. The sacred building's narrow escape and the destruction of the mission's original documentation—along with rumors that go back centuries and span many nations of secret, hidden Jesuit treasure—seem to have given rise to the site's aura of inscrutability.

Never mind—the plan was hatched—I was on my way. I had crossed a conceptual boundary.

Passing between the United States and Mexico has long been commonplace for me. I have traveled to Mexico since I was eight years old, when my family began making regular trips to Ensenada to sail and swim. When I was in college, friends and I would go to Tijuana on Sunday afternoons to see the bullfights and the famous matadors who had arrived from as far away as Spain. The music, the tradition, the ritual, the heat, the crowd—there was nothing like it in Los Angeles, not in the world I came from. Later, I entered the Baja 500 and

04

04
Driving this vehicle, the second
race car I built, I won first place
in Class 2 in the Baja 1000 and
Baja 500.

05
Local fans gather around in the
pit after the 1975 Baja 1000.

Baja 1000 races with a race car I had built, winning my category twice and getting to know the peninsula well, if mainly at high speed.

Despite all of these experiences, every single time I make the crossing, I find the passage from one country, one culture, to the other to be staggering. Everything changes. For me, Mexico is familiar and exotic, accessible and out of reach.

By the time I got to Chihuahua and saw Iglesias San Miguel de Satevó, I had already visited many other Mexican sacred and secular places and had learned more about what those differences meant. I had deepened my appreciation for Mexican culture, with its awe-inspiring sophistication in town planning, art, and architecture at all points in its history. My trip took me south out of Los Angeles, through Baja California's parched and often otherworldly desert, then via ferry across the Sea of Cortés to the mainland. There I toured Mexico's nineteenth-century colonial cities, with their marvelously orna-mented Mexican Baroque buildings and sociable plazas. Those public spaces offered wonderful design lessons, applicable to my own work, in how to accommodate diverse experiences and activities—sun, shade, music, shopping, sitting, eating, and meditating.

Much of the United States has been built around the automobile and a population that expects to use vehi-cles to go places, do its work, and deliver its goods. In contrast, the traditional Mexican cities were made for walkers, and today's Mexican people still use the historic centers as communal meeting places. As we in the United States seek to make our cities and towns more people friendly, the Mexican plazas offer helpful and inspiring direction. They show us, among other things, how people access and make use of public spaces and how they move from one to another.

Figuring this out was a lot of fun. On a square in Oaxaca, I spent hours listening to marimba bands, feel-ing utterly at peace. My family and I joined in the dancing on the plaza at Zacatecas, while in Guanajuato we fol-lowed the crowds celebrating the Feast of Our Lady of Guadalupe. In both cities, we were apparently the only foreigners around. All the other participants seemed to be Mexican. We would ask, "When is the high season?" thinking we would find out when tourists tended to arrive. "This is it!" people would tell us. "The world needs to know about these places," I told myself.

I then saw Monte Albán and other ancient sites. Without their original populations moving about and living their lives, they appear today as monumental sculp-ture—austere, formal, motionless. The colossal construc-tions obviously supported ceremonial activities like ritual and procession, but I couldn't readily visualize where the habitations had been constructed, where the markets had been set up, where other aspects of daily life had occurred. I didn't care. The places were knockout gorgeous, and that was a starting point for further exploration.

My observations in Mexico exposed me to centuries of thought-provoking architecture and town planning. The Mexican locales also significantly altered my understanding of the history of the American West. The people of Mexico have innovated for so long and on such a glorious scale that I began to see how new and how basic many of our efforts north of the border were at comparable points in time. In 1849, according to an account of a nineteenth-century adventurer who visited San Francisco, the city's most powerful man was a saloon owner and the most important woman was the madam of the largest brothel. San Francisco may now be one of our great cities, but in that era it was a tiny, lawless shantytown.

Meanwhile, Mexico already had well-established cities replete with refined architecture, universities, and cathedrals. Nor were they its first cities. Nearly three and a half centuries before, in 1519, when Spanish conquistador Hernán Cortés encountered Moctezuma II, the

06
View of Monte Albán from the South Platform.

06

Aztec ruler presided over a far-flung network of tribute-paying city-states, which he governed from his capital in Tenochtitlan, with its temples, ball courts, and water- and flower-filled pleasure gardens.

When the Spanish arrived in what we know today as Mexico, it had an indigenous population of some seventeen million people, scholars have estimated. Some were settled agricultural populations that had, over something like five thousand years, domesticated an immense number of plants for food and medicine and bred innumerable varieties of the crops that sustain and delight the world today: corn, beans, squash, chilies, tomatoes, chocolate, and more. The first four—corn, beans, squash, and chilies—dominated peasant cuisine of the time, and still do today.

However, the sixteenth-century Aztec nobility used these and much more to throw extravagant banquets, says food historian William Dunmire. In Gardens of New Spain, Dunmire reports that a Franciscan priest, Bernardino de Sahagún, was invited to a banquet in Tenochtitlan and recorded ten paragraphs' worth of elaborate dishes, including fowl accompanied by toasted corn and lobster with chilies, tomatoes, and ground squash seeds. These sound as though they could pass muster in a modern restaurant, though some of the items on the banquet's extensive menu, such as winged ants flavored with savory herbs and locusts with chia, would not appeal to all modern tastes—certainly not mine.

The rugged Baja California peninsula supported a very different culture from that of Moctezuma's people, writes Edward W. Vernon in his handsome photo-essay, "Las Misiones Antiguas." As many as fifty thousand members of hunting and gathering tribes pursued Baja's sparse food sources in what scholars describe as a continual and thereby sustainable seasonal round. The Baja tribes had no settled agriculture, no domesticated animals, and almost nothing in terms of built environment— hardly more than stone sleeping circles. They apparently changed location every few days in their incessant search for food and water, says Vernon.

This scarcity contrasts sharply with other aspects of their culture including: elaborate tattoos, hairstyles, and other personal adornment; finely made basketry, weapons, and ceremonial objects; complex clan relationships; and languages that were highly differentiated, even when groups lived in fairly close proximity, says a leading authority on Baja, Harry W. Crosby, in his book Antigua California. Especially amazing are the region's spectacular Paleolithic cave paintings— now UNESCO World Heritage Sites. They are as mystifying today as when Jesuits first saw them in the 1700s. Who made

07

08

07
Newly restored Iglesias San
Miguel de Satevó, in the mainland state of Chihuahua, sits
above a graceful suspension
bridge over Río Batopilas.

08
Among the many prehistoric
indigenous cave paintings in Baja
are these from Cueva Pintada.
Photo: Glenn Jensen.

them and the artists' connections to the tribes the Jesuits encountered are still to be established, writes Crosby in The Cave Paintings of Baja California. He describes the murals as "dazzling" works that range from realistic to abstract and adhere to formal artistic conventions. This includes a distinctive type of skewed perspective and a vocabulary of grids, stripes, and other devices for filling in figures' outlines.

However, little of sophistication we now see in the paintings, basketry, innumerable dialects, and survival ability was apparent to the first Europeans who met the itinerant inhabitants of Baja. To the new arrivals from Europe, the tribes could not have seemed more primitive—or more in need of being saved. The padres who evangelized the peninsula transformed its land and people. Much of what they created is lost, though some of their churches remain as testaments to their courage, determination, and faith. In the next chapter, I will look at these and at their lasting architectural achievement.

Throughout this trip, I used watercolor, among other media, to record the locales I visited and the people I met. The process of creating watercolors has long been pleasurable to me, while being an excellent way to convey information. I feel that a painting or a sketch allows the viewer great freedom of imagination. It lets viewers bring themselves to the image—to envision themselves in that place, seeing those things, participating in those events, meeting those people. In contrast, photographs tend to record what is obvious and offer information that's useful but not as interactive.

The following pages also include computer drawings. Their bird's-eye views provide a twenty-first-century omniscient perspective, as they assemble and present information that no one can see. In a sense, they are the opposite of the paintings' and drawings' experiential manner of analyzing and communicating. It is my hope that taken all together, these pages and their varied viewpoints will inspire the reader to think in a fresh manner about not just the places described here but all our built environments.

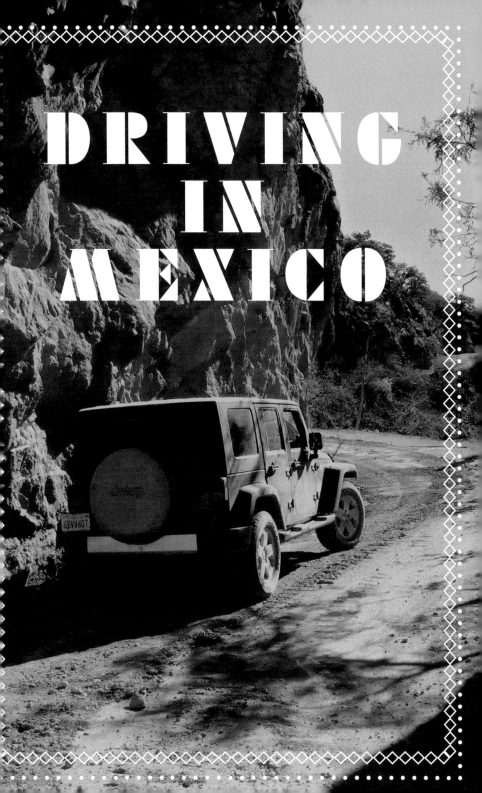

DRIVING
IN
MEXICO

09 (previous page)
The main road leading into Batopilas, in the state of Chihuahua.

10
A memorial dedicated to a truck driver who lost his life on Federal Highway 1, south of El Rosario.

Some features of Mexican road travel may startle foreign visitors. These include the inspection roadblocks between the country's various states, along with surprise military checkpoints. Expect young masked soldiers armed with automatic weapons to inspect your entire vehicle and all your belongings. Apparently, the masks keep the soldiers' identities protected from drug traffickers. They also undoubtedly function to intimidate travelers. At one stop, the soldiers removed every single item from my jeep.

Before you go, you will probably hear rumors that in situations like this, drugs could be planted in the vehicle. I kept a nervous lookout, and it never occurred. When stopped, be prepared to produce the tourist card and other documents, including proof of Mexican car insurance, that you had to obtain to drive into the country. Comply politely with these requests, and do not attempt to bribe federal police.

More reassuring is the excellent condition (though not on Baja) of many Mexican highways. The best ones are toll roads that are as good as anything we have in the United States—safe, well-maintained routes that connect major cities and have clean, well-equipped gas stations and rest stops.

11

11
At roadblocks, young federal police officers with automatic weapons wear masks to protect their identities. The roadblocks are at every state line, but sometimes occur randomly in other locations.

12 (next page)
Police on motorbikes outside of Oaxaca.

Secondary and rural roads are rougher, sometimes just dirt tracks, with intermittent travel facilities. You may not find gas stations for long stretches. It's also possible that you find a station, but it has run out of gas (including those on major highways). To forestall problems, keep your tank as full as possible at all times. You must absolutely avoid night travel on back roads, as animals, unlit vehicles, bicyclists, and even sleeping people may occupy the pavement. In small towns, you will find speed bumps that are so sharply raised, you must slow to nearly a standstill to avoid damaging your vehicle.

In the end, I was glad I chose to make the trip in a four-wheel-drive jeep with a relatively long wheelbase. It was just right for these varied challenges, handling both off-road and highway travel comfortably for up to four people.

13

13
A road heading down the
Baja Peninsula passes through
the south side of Ensenada.

14

These sketches represent the three scales of spaces I saw in Mexico, which are treated in this book in three separate chapters. At the small end of the scale are the individual buildings, such as the missions of Baja California. Next is the middle scale typical of Mexican colonial cities, with their lovely, pedestrian-friendly sequences of spaces. At the large end of the scale are the monumental ancient cities of Mexico, which can be reimagined as living cities.

Movement is a characteristic of architecture. In small churches such as those mentioned above, the architect reinforces the journey from the material world to the spiritual realm with the placement of plazas and doorways, the location of the baptismal font, the entry into the nave, and other means.

In a city, the movement may be choreographed to take the inhabitant or visitor from tight alleys and passages to beautifully open urban spaces and thus provide a sense of delight. This is apparent in Mexico's colonial cities and, if you look hard enough, in its ancient cities as well. In those I visited, avenues and passages led from markets and residential areas to grand plazas.

These characteristics of a building or a city do not just happen, though. They were, and are, determined by architects, builders, and planners.

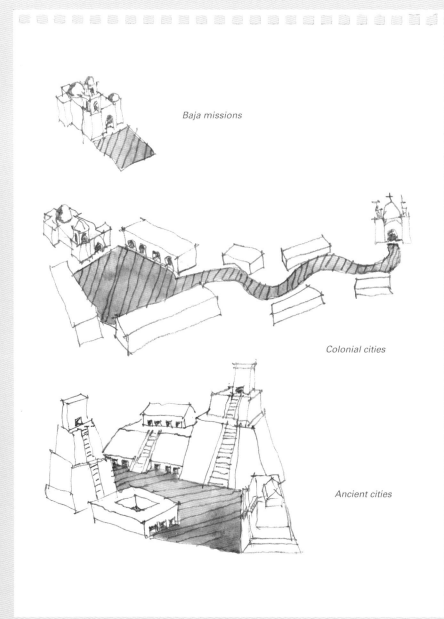

Baja missions

Colonial cities

Ancient cities

BAJA
AND
BEYOND

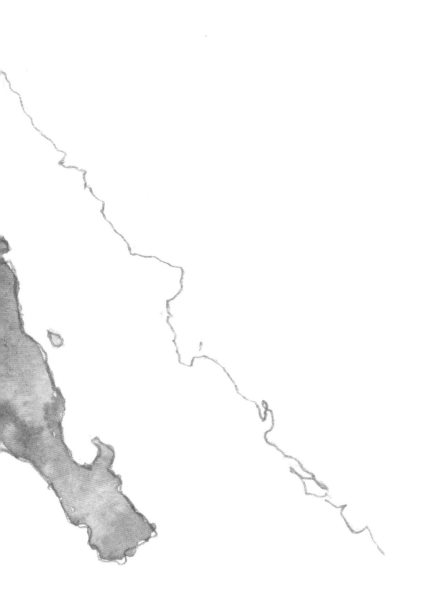

During the 1970s, my father and I raced his sloop along the eight-hundred-mile-long Baja California Peninsula. The coastline we saw was little changed since Spanish treasure ships sailed these waters on their way back and forth to the Philippines, which Spain had claimed in 1521. The ships were transporting Mexican silver east and returning with cargos of Asian spices and silks and other exotic goods. At the time, the peninsula was mistakenly thought to be an island. It was named *California* after a fabulously rich fictional isle ruled by female warriors that figured in an early sixteenth-century Spanish adventure novel.

Off Baja, Dad and I survived the same occasional violent storms that had plagued the so-called Manila Galleons, reefing our sails and riding out the bad weather as their crews probably did. Four and a half centuries after the Spaniards plied these waters, the rocky shore was still wild and remote, with small coves and occasional sandy stretches. At least we didn't have to worry about Francis Drake and the other English, Dutch, and French pirates who preyed on the heavily laden Spanish vessels.

Along with Spanish domination of Baja California and other newly claimed lands came new souls for the Catholic Church. In the days of the divine right of kings, sovereigns were eager for the heavenly rewards as well as the riches they would reap when conquering foreign lands. However, with military and civil authorities in charge of colonization, local populations suffered horribly. In northern New Spain, which encompasses what we now know as Mexico, along with southern and western portions of the United States, indigenous people were felled in the millions. They succumbed to massacres, slave labor in mines and on ranches, and epidemics of smallpox, measles, and other imported diseases to which they had no immunity.

During the 1600s, padres of the Society of Jesus, or Jesuits, devised a novel plan for extending Spanish influence while protecting native converts. Experienced mission builders, Padre Eusebio Francisco Kino and Padre

Baja California

Juan María de Salvatierra, understood Spain's eagerness to harvest the rich pearling beds of Baja California and to acquire a harbor there as a safe haven for provisioning the Manila galleons. However, early military-led attempts to colonize the area had failed miserably. Kino, who had participated in just such a disaster, and his fellow northern Italian, Salvatierra, thought they could do better.

The Society of Jesus was an influential evangelizing order, founded in 1540 by Ignatius of Loyola, a Spanish former knight who put together a streamlined, disciplined organization—more efficient and ambitious than the venerable medieval religious orders with their settled ways, according to Harry Crosby in *Antigua California*. The new order attracted well-educated aristocrats, among others. They were devout, dedicated, and fearless, writes Crosby. They would go anywhere and take on any challenge, no matter how demanding or dangerous, and Spain's rulers liked that.

The order as a whole would have its ups and downs over succeeding centuries, but the reputation of its members as courageous "soldiers of Christ" persisted. Its priests would eventually have star turns as brainy, Bible-toting buccaneers in novels, movies, and (brace yourself) comic books. A Jesuit father provided commentary on the comedy news spoof *The Colbert Report*. Meanwhile, science-fiction treatments have included *The Sparrow*, a book fondly referred to by sci-fi aficionados as "Jesuits in space." More seriously, in the Oscar-winning film *The Mission*, Jeremy Irons stars as an eighteenth-century Jesuit priest who fights to protect his South American Guaraní Indian flock from slavers, including a repentant one played by Robert De Niro. Martin Scorsese optioned *Silence*, a work of historical fiction about the order's travails in seventeenth-century Japan.

The current pontiff, who is the first Jesuit to hold that post, is another media-friendly independent thinker in that tradition. In addition to taking on controversial issues, Pope Francis has appeared with young parishioners in the first-ever papal selfie, paid his own hotel bill, and washed the feet of prison inmates, including a woman, another historical first. In 2013, *Time* magazine named him Person of the Year and *Esquire* dubbed him Best Dressed Man for his simplified papal garb.

Society of Jesus members came from several European countries and the New World. They included urbane intellectuals who tended to be surprisingly open-minded for their day. Admittedly, in Spain's earliest years in the New World, the conquistadores and their entourage had shown some interest in local customs. Bernardino de Sahagún's writing, including his recollection of an Aztec banquet described in the previous section, is an example. Soon though, curiosity about native culture waned and gave way to the notion that it should be eliminated. Many believed the indigenous people were little different from animals, which handily excused slavery, rape, and other brutalities to which they were subjected.

In contrast, the Society of Jesus retained a "guarded acceptance" of the natives, writes scholar and translator Daniel T. Reff in his introduction to the seventeenth-century Jesuit masterwork *History of the Triumphs of Our Holy Faith Amongst the Most Barbarous and Fierce Peoples of the New World*.

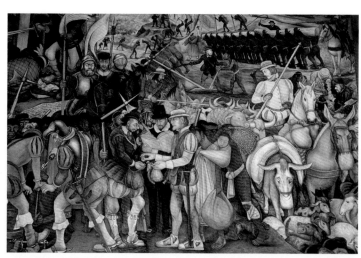

15

The author of the 1645 tome was Andrés Pérez de Ribas, a missionary in Sinaloa and Sonora and later the provincial, or director, of the Jesuit's Province of New Spain. According to Reff, Pérez de Ribas described natives as heathens who were nevertheless "descendants of Adam," like Europeans; it was isolation rather than lack of reason that accounted for their "foolish" and "barbarous" behavior. They needed to be saved, not worked to death or simply exterminated.

Over the course of negotiations during the 1690s, Jesuit padres Eusebio Francisco Kino and Juan María de Salvatierra promised the Spanish crown's viceroy, or deputy, in Mexico City that they would find private patrons to fund the colonization of California. The royal treasury wouldn't risk a peso to acquire all that territory, with its pearling beds and much-needed harbors. In return, the Jesuits wanted to be in charge of the soldiers who would accompany them as protection against hostile tribes. Though few settlers were interested in the California desert, the padres also wanted assurance that they would be allowed to exclude them altogether. From experience, the fathers knew that settlers would compete for native labor and would likely be a poor moral influence. The viceroy agreed to the Jesuits' terms, essentially allowing them to create a theocracy.

In 1697, Salvatierra and a tiny band of soldiers and Christianized mainland natives set sail for California and the task of finding sites that had both enough local people to convert and sufficient water to support the European-style agriculture and villages envisioned. By establishing productive mission sites, they hoped to entice Baja's hunter-gatherers with continually available food. They would then convert tribal members to Christianity, European customs, and a sedentary village life.

In the end, Baja's harsh environment largely defeated most ambitions of agricultural self-sufficiency, and many missions required continual inputs of provisions from the mainland. Nor were all natives convinced

16

16
Prehistoric aboriginal cave paintings can be seen at Cueva Pintada, in Baja. Photo: Glenn Jensen.

that the new lifeways were an improvement; some stayed, but others came and went or even attacked the missions. Those who stayed eventually lost their foraging skills and in lean times were unable to supplement their diets by hunting or gathering. The Baja landscape had become as alien to them as it was to the Spaniards.

Other Jesuits eventually joined Salvatierra. Some missions the Jesuits built over the ensuing decades were moved a few times, and a few lasted just a short period. In all, the order set up nearly twenty missions, along with additional *visitas* (smaller related establishments), in the southern two-thirds of the peninsula. Today the early adobe buildings—churches, dwellings, storerooms, and more—are largely in ruins or have entirely melted away, though some of the irrigation and water-storage systems still function to this day. Eight stone churches survive, some built by the Jesuits and others constructed or finished by the religious orders that succeeded them.

Making Baja California's Churches

From this point, I visited four Baja mission churches. From north to south, they were Misión San Francisco de Borja Adac, Misión San Ignacio de Kadadaamán, Misión Santa Rosalía de Mulegé, and Misión San Francisco Javier de Viggé-Biaundó. I then left the peninsula, taking a ferry to the mainland to find the church of another Jesuit mission, Iglesias San Miguel de Satevó, in the state of Chihuahua.

Today the Baja stone churches appear unusual because they are remote—some extremely so. They sit alone in a hostile landscape. But when they were built, they were part of a complex of adobe dwellings, workshops, and storehouses, along with courtyards where people gathered, shared meals, sang, and prayed. Those adobe outbuildings are now gone or in ruins, giving the impression of greater isolation than when the churches sheltered groups of congregants.

To make the churches more welcoming and meaningful, their builders embellished them both inside and out. The experience of visiting a Baja church is full and complex. Everywhere there is something for the eye to light on and the mind to consider. The decorations reflect the changing styles of Spanish architecture of the time. These included Gothic, Renaissance, Mannerist, and Moorish elements, among others—at least as they were understood in the far reaches of the New World. The iconography of the Catholic Church, the Spanish crown, and wealthy patrons abounds, reminding the visitor of who and what funded the missions.

Everywhere is the influence of the Baroque, a curvilinear style that sought to amaze the viewer with its opulence and drama. This exuberance was thought at the time to be effective in drawing converts to the Catholic Church and, importantly, for luring back those who had deserted to the Reformation's new Protestant sects. The Baroque was, in effect, a marketing tool of the Counter-Reformation.

The Jesuits were on the leading edge of the Church's renewals and reforms during this era and were

THRILL RIDES

17 (previous page)
Boojum trees flourish near Cataviña, in central Baja.

18
Hussong's Cantiña, in Ensenada, was once infamous. During Cinco de Mayo celebrations, police would park out front and walk drunks right into a paddy wagon, or Black Maria.

When traveling by car from the U.S. state of California to Mexico's Baja California, I like to make a hard right after I cross the border in Tijuana in order to get onto a route that leads directly out of town. Making that turn was especially important on this trip. Just weeks before, several people had been found, shot dead, in the center of Tijuana. Well, I missed the turn, and that gave me a good scare. However, I soon found my way back to the road I intended and, without any further mishaps, began driving south on the Transpeninsular Highway, or Federal Highway 1.

In this portion of Baja, the thoroughfare traces its way along the Pacific Ocean, passing occasional sun-bleached and often rundown resorts. It's a challenging two-lane road with lots of curves and huge trucks racing up to the United States with loads of fruits and vegetables. For 60 miles, you will rarely see another person, except for those aggressive truck drivers. Then you hit Ensenada, an industrial port town where cruise ships call and disgorge their passengers for day trips. After an overnight stay there, I continued south on the highway, passing through occasional dusty villages before I arrived in El Rosario 150 miles later. Here, the road swings inland, or east. The habitations thin out, and I became vividly aware of sun and nature and beauty.

19

19
Near Cataviña, in the Parque
Natural del Desierto Central de
Baja California, a protected area
stretches from the Pacific Ocean
to the Sea of Cortés.

Suddenly, I was surrounded by a forest of towering, spindly boojum trees—like tall, misshapen candles. I had entered into the Valle de los Cirios, or Valley of the Candles. It's a protected area that, together with the neighboring wildlife refuge, Reserva de la Biosfera El Vizcaíno, stretches across the peninsula from the Pacific Ocean in the west to the Sea of Cortés in the east and encompasses about a third of Baja's territory. The landscape's strangeness and extravagant beauty brought back wonderful memories. At the town of Cataviña, with its spectacular rock formations and exotic vegetation, I recalled that my wife and I first visited here in 1973. It was a year after the newly finished Transpeninsular Highway opened Baja to more travelers. The government had just completed a series of paradors, or luxury hotels, to attract visitors and to provide sanctuary from the rigors of the gorgeous, but demanding, desert environment.

A few years later, I was back, participating in road races in vehicles I built myself. I first saw the boojum forest in the middle of the night during the Baja 1000. My roof-mounted off-road lights were the only source of illumination on the dirt road. As I rocketed through the Valle de los Cirios, the road got narrower and the boojum trees taller—eerie glowing silhouettes against the black sky. It remains the most thrilling drive of my life.

20

Inhabitants of Baja. Photos: Cardon cactus: iStock.com/Alexander Dunkel; desert fox: iStock.com/bebecom98; brown pelican: iStock.com/kojihirano; barrel cactus, prickly pear cactus: iStock.com/26ISO; puma: iStock.com/anankkml; agave: iStock.com/Videowok_art; harbor seal: iStock.com/KGrif; eastern king snake: iStock.com/GlobalP; boojum: iStock.com/Sam Camp.

This time, I got to appreciate the area at slower speed and in daylight. It was still exciting, though in a quieter way. According to the international conservation group Wildcoast/Costasalvaje, the varied coast-to-coast environment shelters creatures as diverse as mountain lions, desert foxes, harbor seals, and California pelicans. Part of the region, says the conservation group, is an important segment of the Pacific Flyway, a chain of habitats that provide stops for birds migrating along a route that stretches from Alaska to the southern tip of Chile. Some of the plants are unique to this landscape. All around me were not just boojum trees but gnarled elephant trees, rosette-shaped yuccas, spiny barrel cacti, and examples of the cardon, the world's largest cactus, which can top sixty feet.

Cardon cactus

Brown pelican

Desert fox

Barrel cactus

Boojum

Puma

Agave

Eastern king snake

Harbor seal

Prickly pear cactus

21

During the Baja 1000, I felt my vision sharpen as I drove at night and at high speed through the Valle de los Cirios. The boojum trees and cactus, visible in the car's high-powered projector lights, seemed to close in over the narrow course.

22

In this exploded axonometric diagram of Misión San Francisco Javier de Viggé-Biaundó, in the village of San Javier, A shows the shallow arch over the nave, while B represents the center of the cruciform plan supporting the thirty-foot-diameter dome. C is a partial view of the thick walls supporting the vertical weight of the dome and roof and stabilizing against lateral loads caused by wind and earthquakes.

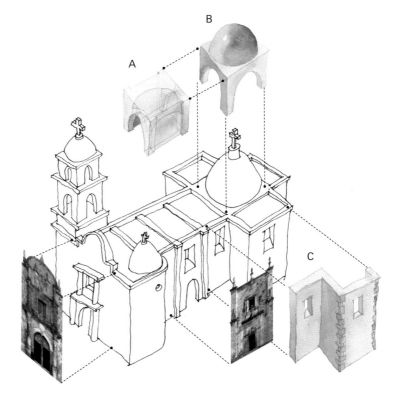

22

42
43

well aware of the different architectural vocabularies and their uses. They applied the Baroque enthusiastically in Baja. For any given church, they appear to have had some decorative items fabricated locally, while importing others from mainland workshops that supplied churches, says Gloria Fraser Giffords, in her marvelously detailed work *Sanctuaries of Earth, Stone, and Light.*

When I look at the construction of the Baja churches, I see aesthetic understanding and a certain amount of technical expertise. I also see similarities among the churches that indicate possible use of a pattern book, along with structural choices that are remarkably similar to indigenous architecture I have seen around the Mediterranean, including in Italy and Spain and across North Africa. There are so many commonalities, one could speculate that the southern European religious that dominated Baja's Jesuit community brought with them these ideas about constructing a sacred space.

Places of worship in both the Mediterranean region and Baja may be made of locally gathered stone, with thick, rubble-filled rock walls pierced by small windows. Such walls can absorb the thrust of the flattened arches that are used to span the interior. Refined stone surrounds and strengthens corners and openings. Domes are small. Lack of timbers that were long enough to cross a wide opening means that spans are narrow—generally twenty-five to thirty feet.

Floor plans in either region may be rectangular or cruciform. Two of the Baja churches I visited—Misión Santa Rosalía de Mulegé and Misión San Francisco de Borja Adac—have flattened arches supporting a long barrel vault (like a horizontal half-cylinder) above a rectangular nave, which is the main body of the church. At Misión San Francisco Javier de Viggé-Biaundó, Misión San Ignacio de Kadadaamán, and Iglesias San Miguel de Satevó, the flattened arches support a dome that surmounts a cross-shaped floor plan.

According to Giffords, the record indicates that the priests imported skilled masons, stonecutters, carpenters, and other artisans from the mainland. The padres themselves appear to have served in varied roles, from designer to manual laborer, depending on their knowledge and what the project required, Giffords says. The improvisatory composition of the team that was responsible for each church, as well as the variability in the type of materials that could be found locally, mean each building grew in an organic fashion. There must have been a certain amount of trial and error and some guesswork and experimentation based on past experience in similar circumstances.

When we build with standardized modern materials, we can readily calculate the forces borne by each element of the construction. The process is rational and predictable. In contrast, we would need to construct a three-dimensional finite-element model, using advanced computational analysis, to understand how the gravitational and lateral forces flow through Baja's stone structures. The churches appear simple, but in fact, what is going on structurally is exceptionally complex.

What is clear is that the makers of Baja's churches acknowledged both the possibilities and the limitations of available materials. They couldn't build wide, so they went long, high, and narrow—surrounding worshipers with a sense of intimacy and community while reaching upward to the heavens.

23

Many Mediterranean vernacular buildings, including these in a Tunisian village, have simple shallow arches, barrel vaults, and domes built without timber. Their construction systems and materials are strikingly similar to those used in Baja's stone churches.

Misión San Francisco de Borja Adac

An axonometric view of Misión San Francisco de
Borja Adac shows the elements of its cruciform plan,
with a barrel vault over the nave but no central dome.

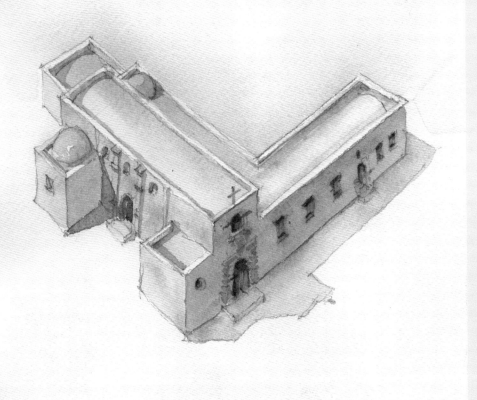

24

BAJA AND BEYOND / MISIÓN SAN FRANCISCO DE BORJA ADAC

Watercourse

Jesuit ruins

Misión San Francisco de Borja Adac

Camino Real

Jesuit orchard walls

N

lat 28°44'39.7" N, long 113°45'15.3" W

Misión San Francisco de Borja Adac

100 ft.

The northernmost of the Jesuit missions, Misión San Francisco de Borja Adac was founded in 1762. It was named for an early leader of the Society of Jesus, to which the native place name, Adac, was appended. Jesuits founded the mission itself, though Dominicans built the stone church, finishing it in 1801. Found after driving down a rough dirt track, this mission, more than any other, exemplifies remoteness. It exudes a sense of dire unsuitability for anything settled, much less a thriving agricultural community. The church is severe, with chiseled frontier-Baroque ornamentation of windows and doors. From this austerity derives its great beauty.

The Mexican government has refurbished this and other Baja churches through the historic preservation program of its Instituto Nacional de Antropología e Historia, or INAH. However, when I first saw San Francisco de Borja in 1973, it was utterly abandoned. I found the spot after jolting down the terrible road and asking directions from men I later realized were part of a prison work gang. I worked my way cautiously from room to room, hoping as I did so that the floor would not cave in nor would the ceiling collapse. I saw a blood spatter on a wall. All the while, I wondered how the makers of this church and others like it had survived in this forbidding wilderness and, while doing so, had created arresting, brilliant, and lasting architecture.

Misión San Francisco
de Borja Adac

25

The south elevation of Misión San Francisco de Borja Adac shows the main entry leading into the worship space. The doorway is surmounted by symbols of the Dominican Order and of the church's patron, the House of Borja. An upper opening brings light to the choir loft. Photo: Antonella Carri/REDA&CO.

26
The south elevation of Misión
San Francisco de Borja Adac.
Photo: Antonella Carri/REDA&CO.

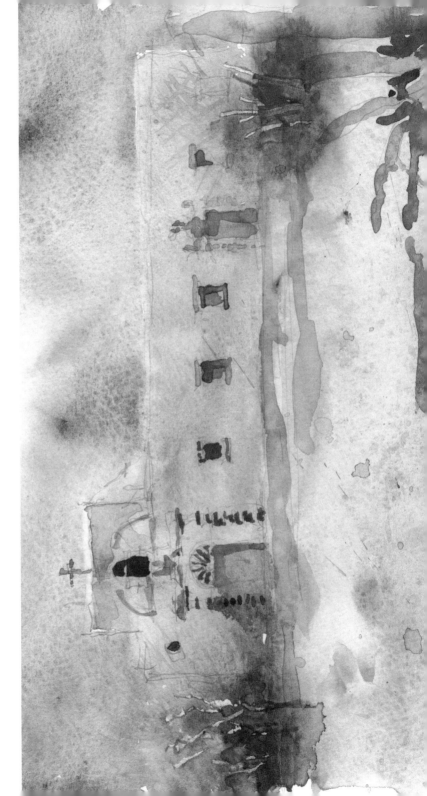

27
Watercolor of the south elevation of
Misión San Francisco de Borja Adac,
as seen from across the plaza.

28
Exterior of the side altar.

SAN FRANCISCO de BORJA

29

29

The elemental floor plan of Misión San Francisco de Borja Adac includes the main worship space, nave, and transept to the left and an administrative space to the right.

Misión San Ignacio de Kadadaamán

The classic plan of a number of the mission churches can be seen in this axonometric view of Misión San Ignacio de Kadadaamán, in the town of San Ignacio. There is a bell tower to the left of the entry. A cross axis along the front adds structural strength to the building and, in the interior, accommodates the baptismal font on one side and the stairway to the choir loft on the other. The cruciform wing crosses the nave, which increases lateral strength and accommodates the dome.

N

Misión San Ignacio de Kadadaamán

Main plaza

100 ft.

lat 27°17'1.9" N, long 112°53'54.6" W

Misión San Ignacio de Kadadaamán

I first saw this church in 1972. San Ignacio de Kada-daamán was another mission that was blessed with a productive site. The Jesuits founded it in 1728, naming it after the primary founder of their order. *Kadadaamán* is a native place name. The padres commenced the stone church in the mid-1700s and worked on it until 1767, their last year on the peninsula.

Apparently little building was done during the transfers of the mission to the Franciscan and then the Dominican Order. The latter finished the church in 1786. Its interior includes a statue of San Ignacio, while an ornate gilded panel behind the altar displays paintings of additional saints. The façade, which faces a square in the town of San Ignacio, is applied in the Mannerist style with a profusion of stone carvings, royal and other coats of arms, and niches for statues; it's capped with bulky, Moorish-type finials.

31
This view of the retablo of Misión San Ignacio de Kadadaamán is from the nave beneath the dome. The gilded panel is the setting for Baroque and Mannerist oil paintings of the eighteenth century, with subjects including the Jesuit Order's founder, Saint Ignatius of Loyola, and the Passion of Christ. Photo: Glenn Jensen.

Misión San Ignacio de Kadadaamán

32

The town of San Ignacio is a palm-filled oasis, with unique flora and fauna in the midst of Baja's arid Central Desert. Springs outside town have supplied it with water since the seventeenth century and, before that, were a water source for indigenous communities.

33

The center of San Ignacio has a heavily shaded central plaza, as well as shops and municipal buildings.

34
The front, or east elevation, of Misión San Ignacio de Kadadaamán may be a bit ill-proportioned and overwrought. However, it is a veritable library of symbols of the eighteenth century.

35
The Spanish royal coat of arms is to the left of the door.
The Dominican coat of arms is above the door. To the right
of the door is a representation of the Pillars of Hercules,
an ancient term for the promontories flanking the Strait of
Gibraltar and indicating the end of the known world; by
placing them here, Spain is redefining them as a gateway
to the wider world.

36

A side entry on the south elevation of Misión San Ignacio de Kadadaamán leads to the churchyard, where I can envision informal social gatherings taking place from the mission's earliest days. Stonework around the doors structurally reinforces the openings and shows expert craftsmanship.

37
The south elevation of Misión San Ignacio de Kadadaamán has an exterior stairway to the choir loft. Here, the smooth plaster of the wall, which was painted to look like masonry, is worn away, revealing the rough stonework beneath.

38
San Ignacio's freshwater lake
and palm grove.

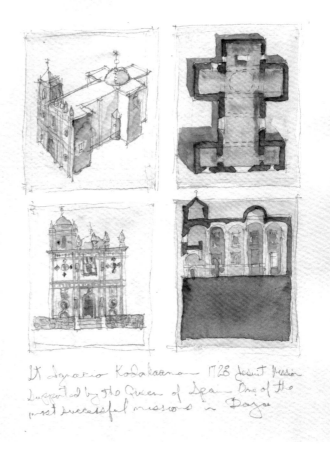

St Ignacio Kadakaaman 1728 Jesuit Mission Supported by the Queen of Spain One of the most successful missions in Baja

39

Clockwise from upper left: an axonometric view, the floor plan, a cross section, and the east elevation of Misión San Ignacio de Kadadaamán.

40

40
The façade of Misión San Ignacio de Kadadaamán faces the town plaza's west side.

Misión Santa Rosalía de Mulegé

This axonometric view shows Misión Santa Rosalía de Mulegé. Today the handsome church structure sits alone on high ground above the palm groves of the town of Mulegé and the river of the same name. In the mission's heyday, it was surrounded by dwelling places for both priests and the natives they had converted, who became part of the Church community. The tower is attached to the left wing, which is constructed with a barrel vault. This wing would have housed the mission's administration activities and could also have been used for storing and protecting supplies, including food. The exposed rusticated volcanic stone gives the structure a sense of purity and strength. I saw no evidence that plastering ever existed on the façade. As with other Baja churches, more intricate stonework surrounds the openings and pilasters.

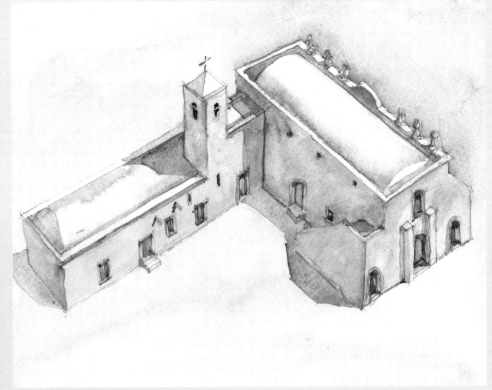

Rio Mulegé

Misión Santa Rosalía de Mulegé

Gathering space

lat 26°53′7.5″ N, long 111°59′10.1″ W

Misión Santa Rosalía de Mulegé

100 ft.

When compared to San Ignacio, Misión Santa Rosalía de Mulegé is stark, even minimalist. Mulegé was yet another well-chosen location: high in the rugged hills above the luxuriant valley of the Río Mulegé. It was first identified by Padre Salvatierra's initial partner in Baja, the Sicilian priest Francisco María Piccolo, who named the site after the twelfth-century patron saint of his native island, writes David Burckhalter in his excellent work *Baja California Missions*.

The Jesuits finished Misión Santa Rosalía's L-shaped church in 1766, according to Burckhalter. They used gray and brown volcanic stone, with thick layers of mortar forming a prominent visual feature on surfaces inside and out. The interior walls, some of which are plastered, were once hung with many paintings. Now lost, they depicted religious scenes and portraits of saints and the mission's founders, says Burckhalter. An eighteenth-century statue of Santa Rosalía remains. She is portrayed in a simple brown robe and with flowers in her hair, raising a hand in benediction as she smiles over the church from a glass case. The sacred building surrounding the statue is similarly humble, honest, and handsomely composed.

42
The south façade of Misión Santa Rosalia de Mulegé, a wing surmounted by a barrel vault, and the tower. Finials march along the east elevation, rather than where they might be expected—over the front entry on the south elevation.

Misión Santa Rosalía de Mulegé

42

43

Restrained landscaping and simple pilasters flank the entry to the nave on the south elevation of Misión Santa Rosalía de Mulegé.

44
Rio Mulegé and a palm-filled oasis below
Misión Santa Rosalía de Mulegé.

45
Watercolor of the south elevation
of Misión Santa Rosalía de Mulegé.

46
The south elevation of Misión
Santa Rosalía de Mulegé.

47

Clockwise from upper left: the axonometric view of Misión Santa Rosalia de Mulegé shows the choir loft's stair tower, the two barrel vaults, and the rooftop finials. The mission's floor plan depicts the central nave and altar, with the administration wing to the west. The south elevation of Misión Santa Rosalia de Mulegé is seen with accompanying notes.

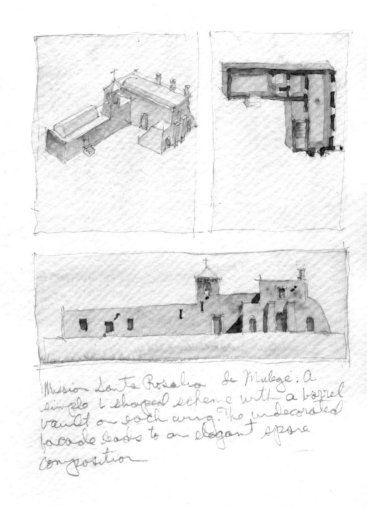

Misión Santa Rosalia de Mulegé: a simple L shaped scheme with a barrel vault on each wing. The undecorated facade leads to an elegant spare composition

48
The bell tower of Misión Santa
Rosalía de Mulegé.

48

Misión San Francisco Javier de Viggé-Biaundó

Set in the tiny village of San Javier, Misión San Javier de Viggé-Biaundó is in a small, fertile valley protected by surrounding mountains. The church's north elevation fronts on a long town plaza. This axonometric view shows the classic cruciform plan of what I believe is the jewel of the Baja missions. Seeing a photograph of it was also, as I described in the preceding chapter, one of the inspirations for this trip and for writing this book. The church was constructed of volcanic stone, which was plastered over at one time. Most of this coating has worn away. In a time-honored manner, the interaction between the mission church and the nearby town is intense and continual, with markets, festivals, and celebrations marking the holy days.

Agricultural fields

Main plaza

Misión San Francisco Javier de Viggé-Biaundó

N

lat 25°51'38.2" N, long 111°32'37.6" W

Misión San Francisco Javier de Viggé-Biaundó

100 ft.

All of the Baja churches I visited were glorious, but the one that had the most impact on me was Misión San Francisco Javier de Viggé-Biaundó. One of the peninsula's earliest missions, it was founded by the Jesuits in 1699. Arriving at the site was like stepping into the photograph that architectural-history professor Carleton Winslow Jr. had snapped here and shown us American architecture students decades ago—the image that launched my trips to Baja California over the years. The mission's stone church was named for a cofounder of the Society of Jesus, along with two native place names. Built from cut blocks of gray volcanic stone between 1744 and 1758, it includes fine stone carvings and intricately ornamented door and window frames. Miraculously, the building has survived, intact, thanks to restoration over the years. It rises above the tiny village of San Javier, about twenty-five miles from Loreto, where Padre Salvatierra established his first mission in 1697.

The surroundings are spectacular, with a rarity on Baja—a lush, well-watered canyon where fields, orchards, and the first vineyard in the Californias were established. An oasis in the midst of an otherwise desolate landscape, it clearly made sense as a mission site. Scholars say it also made sense to the native people of the area, who had taken advantage of its water and other resources, presumably for centuries.

Misión San Francisco
Javier de Viggé-
Biaundó

50
Misión San Francisco Javier
de Viggé-Biaundó in 1973.

51
Market stalls fill a rectangular plaza during the feast of San Javier at Misión San Francisco Javier de Viggé-Biaundó.

52
The west elevation of Misión San Francisco Javier de Viggé-Biaundó includes exuberant Mannerist rooftop finials and detailing at the doors and pilasters.

52

53

Spiral-shaped Baroque-style pilasters flank the choir window on the main façade of Misión San Francisco Javier de Viggé-Biaundó. The pilasters' design takes me back to Bernini's Baldachin, a sculpted canopy with similar columns in Saint Peter's Basilica, in Vatican City.

54
At the main entry on the north elevation of Misión San Francisco Javier de Viggé-Biaundó, some plasterwork remains. However, most of it has worn away, and the volcanic stone beneath is now exposed.

55

On the west elevation of Misión San Francisco Javier de Viggé-Biaundó, the stonework around pilasters and at wall edges is well cut and disciplined in construction, adding both beauty of detail and strength to these critical structural components.

Faith in
Motion

56 (previous page)
Caballero at the feast day of
San Javier at the Misión San
Francisco Javier de Viggé-Biaundó.

57
The main road to the village
of San Javier.

When I got to Misión San Francisco Javier de Viggé-Biaundó, action swirled around the church. It was in the midst of the 307th anniversary of the feast of its saint. As I began to ascend the hill to the church, my jeep became part of an exuberant procession of horsemen dressed in exquisite traditional Spanish costumes, walkers, more drivers in their vehicles, and a man bearing a cross. People carried colorful banners, and a brass band played. Some of the caballeros had clearly been drinking. At one point, police officers stopped me and wanted to know if I were taking beer in. I wasn't, and I later learned that festival participants are required to buy their beer locally.

Once in town, I found a spot to park the jeep and explored market stalls offering a riotous mix of religious articles, household goods, and a whole lot more. In one stall, simple, elegant Spanish-style saddles shared space with undergarments. A steady stream of people flowed in and out of the church, which offered services throughout the day. The high-spirited cavalcade to San Francisco Javier was the first of several processional celebrations that I encountered, participated in, and grew to love during this trip to Mexico. They were thrilling examples of architecture as the setting for pageantry and for prayer.

58
A pilgrim carrying a cross to the feast day of San Javier.

59
More travelers on their way to the mission, followed by family members in SUVs.

61 (next page)
Mannerist and Baroque detailing graces a pilaster.

58

59

60
Pilgrim riding to the feast day of
San Javier.

62
Stonework detailing.

63

63
The mission as seen
from the plaza.

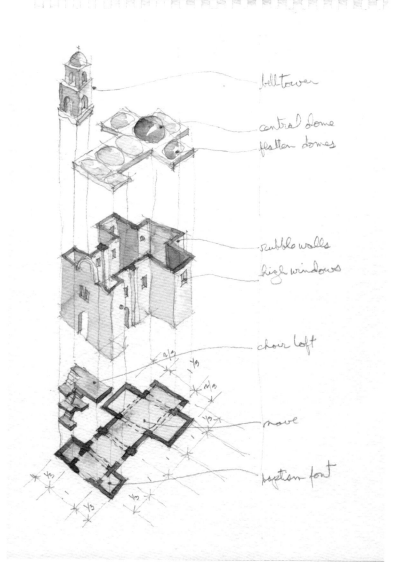

64
An exploded axonometric view of Misión San Francisco Javier de Viggé-Biaundó shows the basic organization of the structure, including the proportions of the structural grid.

bell tower

central dome
flatten domes

rubble walls
high windows

choir loft

nave

baptism font

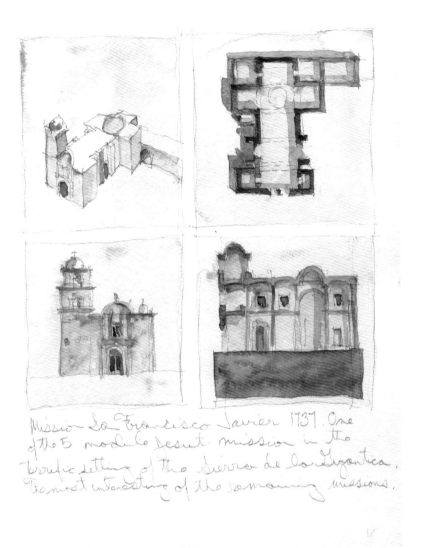

Misión San Francisco Javier 1737. One of the 5 module Jesuit mission in the terrific setting of the Sierra de la Gigantica. The most interesting of the remaining missions.

65
Clockwise from top left: an axonometric view, a floor plan, a cross section, and an elevation of Misión San Francisco Javier de Viggé-Biaundó.

Iglesias San Miguel de Satevó

This axonometric view is of Iglesias San Miguel de Satevó, one of the last Jesuit mission churches. It is near the town of Batopilas, in the mainland state of Chihuahua. The church was finished in 1764, near the end of the Jesuits' tenure in Mexico. As one of the order's later churches, it shows developments from other cruciform-plan structures. The semicircular shape of the apse at the rear and of the cruciform wings, along with additional curved walls and arches, give this church a more fluid and organic character than those in Baja. The four-tiered bell tower also marks the structure as a more complex and exuberant composition than the Baja churches.

Iglesias San Miguel de Satevó

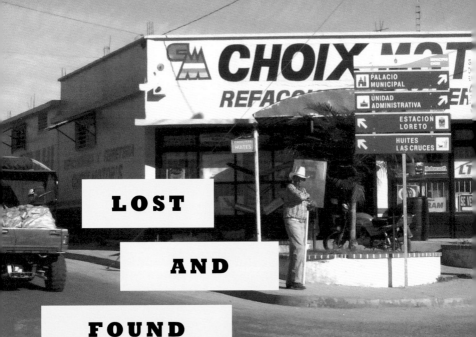

LOST

AND

FOUND

IN CHIHUAHUA

67 (previous page)
Leaving El Fuerte for Batopilas.

68
Tarahumara Indians rescue
me and my jeep.

My guide would find me. That was all I knew when
I loaded my jeep onto a ramshackle ferry and crossed
the Sea of Cortés to El Fuerte ("The Fort"), a town on
Mexico's mainland that's supposedly the hometown
of the historical person who inspired the fictional
Zorro. From El Fuerte, I planned to drive to the colonial mining town of Batopilas, in the nearby state of
Chihuahua. There I would find Iglesias San Miguel
de Satevó, the Jesuit mission church that had turned
out to be neither lost nor last, though it would be the
final one of its type that I would see on this trip.

El Fuerte is so small that any stranger coming
into town is obvious to everyone—just like in old-time
western movies. The center of town is a couple of
blocks with a church, a saloon, and some motels. As a
result, my guide had no problem spotting me. He was
an American with a lovely Mexican wife. She turned
out to be the key to the success of the last leg of my
search for the fabled Jesuit churches.

We headed out, I in my jeep and the guides in
their ATV. The roads from El Fuerte to Batopilas are
rarely more than rough tracks, tracing their way
through soaring crags and gaping valleys. We saw a
few tiny farms, perched on precipitous mountainsides.

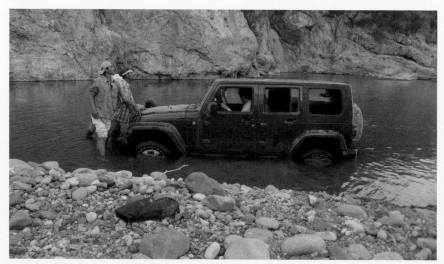

69
Filling up with gasoline.

70 (next page)
Rest stop outside Urique,
a town in Chihuahua.

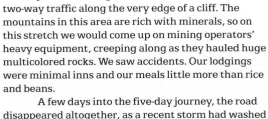

At one point, we navigated a one-lane dirt road with two-way traffic along the very edge of a cliff. The mountains in this area are rich with minerals, so on this stretch we would come up on mining operators' heavy equipment, creeping along as they hauled huge multicolored rocks. We saw accidents. Our lodgings were minimal inns and our meals little more than rice and beans.

A few days into the five-day journey, the road disappeared altogether, as a recent storm had washed it out. Our only choice was proceeding in the river itself. The guide assured me that the shallow parts of the river were safe and clearly indicated by the turbulence of the water. Only the deeper portions of the river were still. If I kept to the churning water, I would be fine. This worked for about five miles, as we lurched down the riverbed, which was hemmed in by high, rugged cliffs. Then I hit a deep spot, and the jeep got stuck. My first thoughts were that the vehicle was a total loss and that we were in big trouble. We were one hundred miles from the last paved road and civilization. The guide's wife said there was a Tarahumara settlement nearby. They went to check, and the next thing I knew, about ten tribal members were racing toward me along the boulder-strewn riverbed.

I am sure you immediately recalled that the Tarahumara are celebrated ultra-long-distance runners who run everywhere. They have famously complained that Olympic marathons and other daunting international contests, which they may run in sandals or even barefoot, are simply too short. They have barely gotten going when the approximately twenty-six miles are over. However, at the moment I saw them dashing in my direction, I did not remember any of this. I was terrified. Things quickly sorted themselves out, and between the Tarahumara men and the winch on the ATV, the jeep was soon free, and I was back on my way to Batopilas.

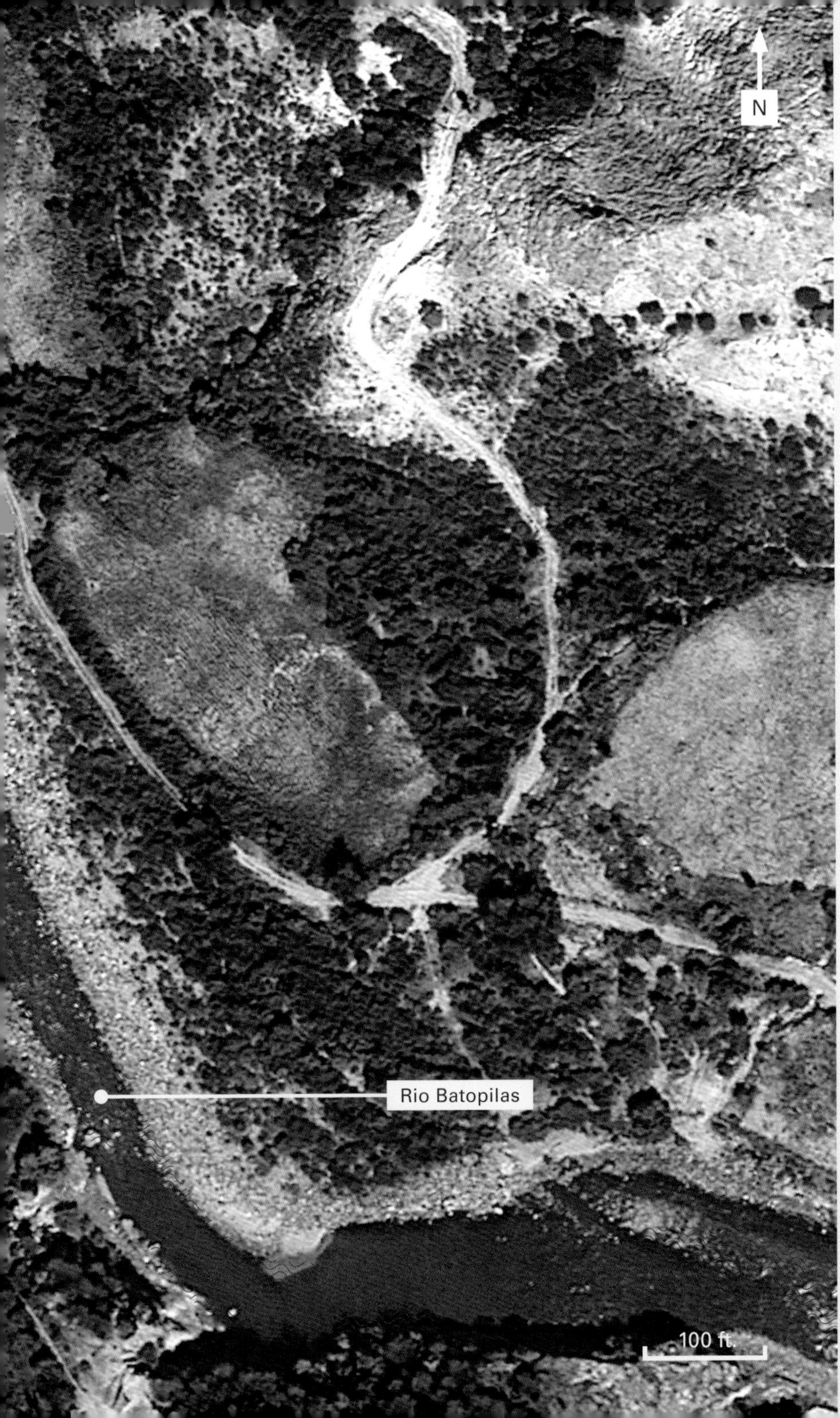

N

lat 26°59'34" N, long 107°42'52" W

Iglesias San Miguel de Satevó

Rio Batopilas

100 ft.

On the Mexican mainland, a few miles south of the colonial mining town of Batopilas in the state of Chihuahua, I saw Iglesias San Miguel de Satevó. The not-really-lost Jesuit mission church was a big part of inspiring this trip. My adventures while searching for it are described in "Lost and Found in Chihuahua." Restored by the Mexican government's Instituto Nacional de Antropología e Historia, Iglesias San Miguel de Satevó is set high above the banks of a river and a picturesque pedestrian bridge.

Like Misión San Ignacio de Kadadaamán, on Baja, San Miguel's floor plan is cruciform. However, unlike the rectilinear San Ignacio, San Miguel has lots of arcs: domes, partial domes, arches, and curved walls. Semicircular shapes form the plans of the side altars and the apse, the portion of a church that contains the main altar. Meanwhile, the walls of the sacristy, where the priest dons his robes, outline a nearly complete circle. The central portion of the façade's roofline is semicircular.

All the rounded lines give San Miguel a pronounced Baroque appearance and a gracious sensuality not found in its Baja counterparts. The churches of Baja may have dominated their surroundings by means of forceful, ascetic lines, but San Miguel stands out in the landscape because of its shapely curves. It dominates its verdant valley with a fulsome composition of cylinders, arcs, and domes.

Iglesias San Miguel
de Satevó

71
The flowing curvilinear forms of the newly renovated Iglesias San Miguel de Satevó are apparent in this view of the north elevation.

71

72

Iglesias San Miguel de Satevó sits above a suspension bridge across Río Batopilas.

73
Iglesias San Miguel de Satevó
in the early morning.

74
Exuberant curvilinear forms of
Iglesias San Miguel de Satevó.

75
An interior view of the baptistery
of Iglesias San Miguel de Satevó.

76

Clockwise from top left: an axonometric
view, the floor plan, and the east elevation
of Iglesias San Miguel de Satevó.

MISSION DE SATEVO   JAN 2008   DLM

The Empire Moves On

The Jesuits' influence in the Spanish empire, including their grand Baja experiment, ended in the late 1760s. Faraway political wrangling transformed the lives of the order's determined priests. A poisonous brew of power struggles within the Church, waning support from the Spanish throne, and rumors that the order had been hoarding great riches in Baja proved devastating to the Society of Jesus. On June 24, 1767, the viceroy of New Spain opened a letter telling him to arrest and expel all Jesuits in Mexico.

The next day, the viceroy began doing so, first on the mainland and later across the Sea of Cortés in Baja California. A Spanish officer and a contingent of soldiers undertook long, grueling marches throughout the peninsula to one far-flung mission after another. They informed the padres at each that their order had been outlawed; their lands and wealth were to be confiscated; and they were "relieved of every responsibility, spiritual and temporal," reports Harry Crosby, in *Antigua California*.

The Jesuits of Baja gathered at Loreto, the site of their first mission, in order to be led under guard to a waiting ship. According to Crosby, native converts sobbed and knelt with their arms flung out, as though they'd been crucified. They clung to their priests. Officials who later inventoried the missions, expecting to find secret treasure, were astonished at their isolation and poverty. No mounds of pearls. No stockpiles of silver. Under the merciless new regime, the entire indigenous population of the southern two-thirds of the peninsula, already depleted by epidemics, was dead by the middle of the next century. Missions were abandoned.

The focus had shifted north. England and Russia were making their presence felt in the region, and Spain needed a new mission chain that would help extend its rule into Alta California. Soldiers and missionaries heading for the new territories included a Franciscan, Padre Junípero Serra, whom I remembered learning about during my own California parochial-school days.

Baja's stone churches are the survivors of this turbulence—enduring reminders of the Jesuits' gallant efforts to carry on what they believed was the unfinished evangelizing work of Christ and his followers. In one of the least promising landscapes on earth, the Jesuits and to a lesser extent their successors in Baja, the Franciscans and the Dominicans, created these sacred places. They made spaces for ritual—for baptism, communion, and the reading of the Gospel. Miles off the paved road, you come around a corner, and with no prelude, a church materializes out of little more than faith—the most gorgeous, the most unlikely building you could imagine, in the middle of nowhere, rich with meaning.

77
The majestic north elevation of Misión San Francisco Javier de Viggé-Biaundó. Photo: Glenn Jensen.

A ROSARY
OF CITIES AND
SPACES

It was December 12, and my wife and I were standing in a plaza in Guanajuato, capitol of the Mexican state of the same name. We were surrounded by a lively, brightly dressed crowd of thousands of kids and adults. The excitement was palpable. It was as though the whole city was vibrating. Then we noticed that people were disappearing into a narrow opening between two buildings on one side of the square.

We exchanged glances. "Let's go! Let's find out what's happening!" we said to each other.

Once we'd passed through the mysterious gap, we were swept along twisting, narrow streets lined with blue, red, orange, and yellow buildings and draped in fluttering pennants in the red, green, and white of Mexico's flag. People explained to us that the event was a celebration of the feast day of Nuestra Señora de Guadalupe—Our Lady of Guadalupe. In 1531, the Virgin Mary appeared as a beautiful woman surrounded by rays of light to a poor Mexican Indian. She spoke to him in his own language and imprinted her image on his poncho. This miraculous appearance eventually led to widespread acceptance of Catholicism by indigenous Mexicans, who had been reluctant to embrace the new faith.

78 (previous page) Guanajuato hillside.

79 Pilgrims journey up narrow, twisting streets to reach a church dedicated to the Virgin of Guadalupe on her feast day in Guanajuato.

The crowd got bigger and noisier, as we all headed for a gaily festooned crimson church dedicated to the Virgin Mary. The processional passed photography stands, where families bought portraits of their children in theatrical settings—wrapped in a serape or seated on a statue of a horse, for example. Other stands sold fruit, jars of honey, and other appropriate gifts for Our Lady.

We arrived at the plaza of the shrine, which was perched on top of a flight of steps and silhouetted against a cloud-flecked azure sky. Boys and young men had climbed the church towers and watched the merriment from the roof. As we entered the white-and-gold interior, the atmosphere changed. People became quiet, reverent. They placed their gifts on a table near the altar, were blessed by the priest, and moved out through a side door.

On the way to the church, the crowd traversed a portion of Guanajuato's rosary of public spaces, with plazas strung together by streets that are the exuberant result of centuries of pedestrian-friendly town planning. Here and in other Mexican cities, I saw not just exceptional examples of urban design but also adaptation to climate and spectacularly beautiful structures, including those decorated in the almost unimaginably ornate Mexican Baroque style. Continual parades, processions, music and dance performances, and pageantry made architecture not just a backdrop for sacred and secular events but an active participant. The built environment directed our attention and movements; provided places to eat, rest, and find shade; and offered alcoves, plazas, and raised areas where entertainers could perform.

Diving into History

The layout and functioning of Mexico's cities—including four of those I visited, Zacatecas, Guanajuato, San Miguel de Allende, and Oaxaca—were shaped by the *Leyes de Indias,* or the Laws of the Indies, decreed by Philip II of Spain on July 13, 1573. The Spanish ruler intended the Laws of the Indies to govern the expanding Spanish Empire, determine the setup of new towns and cities, and regulate the way land and other resources were distributed. The king's directives for a central plaza, perpendicular streets extending from it, streets radiating from each corner, places for merchants and government buildings, prominent placement of the main temple, and more were generally heeded. The royal edict is apparent in towns and cities both north and south of today's United States–Mexico border, including Los Angeles, where I live and work.

There are exceptions, though. Spain was distant from its colonies, and the rules, including those for humane treatment of the local population, could be ignored. In the case of the street plans for Zacatecas and Guanajuato, the divergence from the regulations was inevitable. When Spanish-era mining towns were built over hillsides and/or existing native villages, the Laws of the Indies had to be adapted. As a result, these cities have narrow, steep, twining streets with a Spanish overlay that is less apparent than in recti-linear San Miguel de Allende and Oaxaca.

Important design ideas are apparent in all four cities, each of which is a UNESCO World Heritage Site; Contemporary people use the historic centers as communal space, and ritual and tradition are rooted in the urban places, with processionals and festivals traversing sequences of them.

The Laws of the Indies were inspired by *De architectura*, an extensive and detailed list of requirements for well-made structures and cities drawn up in the first century BC by the Roman architect, civil engineer, and soldier Marcus Vitruvius Pollio. Vitruvius dedicated his thesis on architecture and town planning

80 (opposite)
Philip II of Spain, who in 1573 signed the Laws of the Indies, controlling the expansion of the Spanish Empire.
Library of Congress.

to Augustus Caesar, who became Rome's emperor in 27 BC. In Vitruvius's ten-volume treatise, he advocated constructing individual buildings and entire cities that exhibited *firmitas, utilitas,* and *venustas,* or solidity, usefulness, and beauty.

As Philip II would do centuries later, Vitruvius emphasized the relationship of architecture to the public good. In the introduction to *De architectura,* Vitruvius wrote that after a busy stretch of laying low Rome's enemies, Augustus Caesar was turning his attention to social welfare and public order, along with extensive building projects. Hence, the timing of the publication of Vitruvius's book. He promises his royal patron that the rules laid out in *De architectura* will ensure that the emperor's many achievements endure.

81
Illustration from Vitruvius's
De architectura. Library of Congress.

The Laws of the Indies followed Vitruvius's lead in mandating that the Spanish Empire's new towns and cities would have public squares that accommodated places of worship, markets, and government buildings. Urban areas in hot climates would have narrow streets that cast shade on passersby; in cold areas, the streets would be wider and sunnier. The major house of worship would be set high up, so it could be seen and admired from afar. Potential sources of disease, such as hospitals, slaughterhouses, and tanneries, would be sited downwind. With these and other rules, the new burgs would be comfortable, beautiful, safe, and prosperous. Their eventual expansion would be rational and aesthetically pleasing.

Centuries after Philip II laid down his rules, another grid began its march westward across the American continent, changing it profoundly and eventually meeting up with and overlapping the earlier Spanish grid. The new checkerboard was called the Jeffersonian grid, after its originator, Thomas Jefferson. It was rigid—oriented strictly to the cardinal directions—whereas Philip II's guidelines had taken note of wind and sun in siting towns and their streets. By means of the unforgiving Jeffersonian grid, an immense continent of varied ecosystems and landforms—grasslands, deserts, river bottomlands, rolling hills, and mountains—was divvied up and transformed into real estate parcels that could be readily bought and sold. If you've flown over the Midwest or West or perused a state map from these regions, you've seen this rectilinear lattice. Established by the Land Ordinance of 1785, the Jeffersonian grid later helped the cash-strapped Continental Congress make money by selling off the vast tract acquired through the 1803 Louisiana Purchase.

The Jeffersonian grid is not sensitive to the needs of land or people, as Philip II wanted the Laws of the Indies to be. Contemporary environmentalists have pointed to Jefferson's unyielding framework as a contributor to ecological destruction. It allowed a prospective settler to pick out a tract of faraway land with the idea of making it into a ranch or farm, whether or not it was suited to that use. Making this happen on a continent-wide scale eventually required importing nonnative plants and animals, destruction of native species, vast dam and water projects, and plowing up fragile prairie soils on a grand scale. This led in turn to famous catastrophes, including the Dust Bowl.

To this day, the idea that nature can be forced to do anything if enough inputs are used encourages the use of herbicides, pesticides, fertilizers, and extensive irrigation in order to make crops grow in inappropriate landscapes, such as deserts. It also contributes to urban sprawl by facilitating the development of garish strip-mall-lined highways, big-box stores, and housing subdivisions.

82

Thomas Jefferson's rigid Jeffersonian grid succeeded the Laws of the Indies. The template, seen here applied in Ohio, was imposed on the American continent to ease land transfers. Library of Congress.

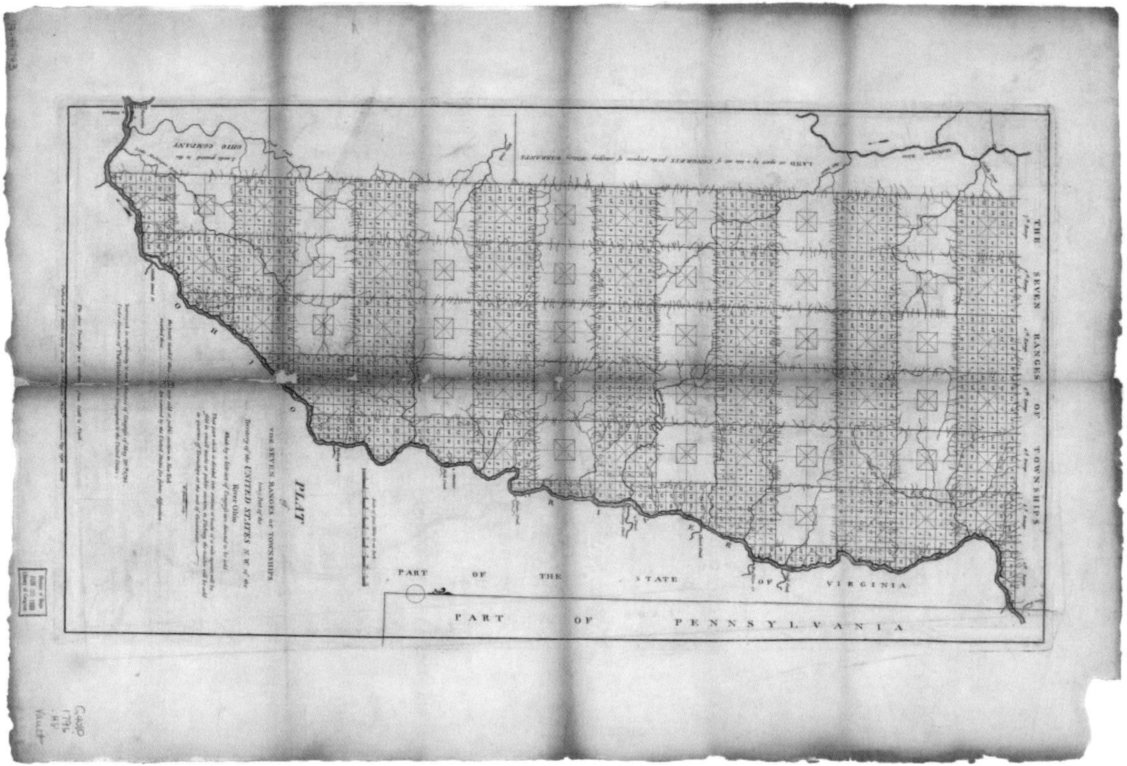

82

ZACATECAS

A. Ópera

B. Iglesia de Santo Domingo

C. Callejón de Gómez Farías

D. Mercado

E. Zócalo

F. Catedral de Zacatecas

Religious buildings

Civic buildings

Sequence of public space

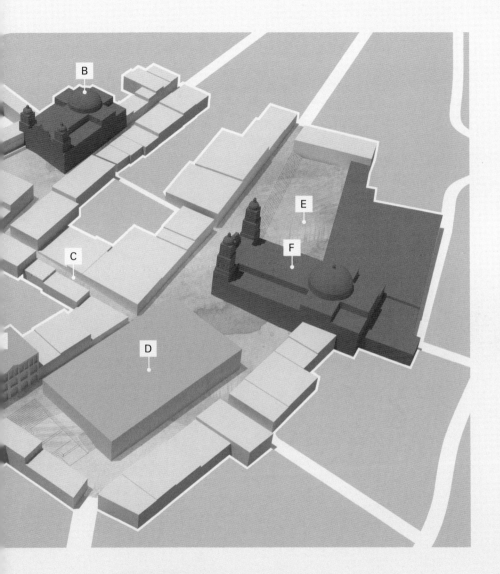

Founded: 1548
Current population: 130,000

Zacatecas started as a mining camp and quickly grew
into a prosperous city. The cityscape was molded to
the irregular topography of the mountainous region.

100 ft.

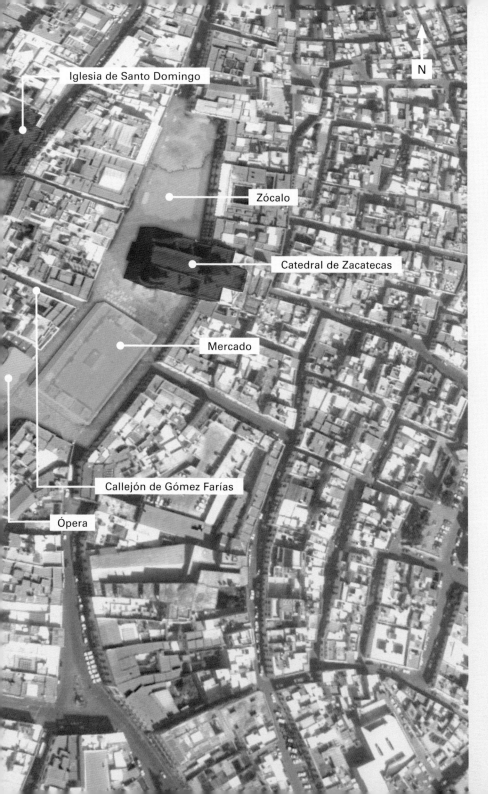

Iglesia de Santo Domingo

Zócalo

Catedral de Zacatecas

Mercado

Callejón de Gómez Farías

Ópera

N

Zacatecas

In my north-to-south trip on the Mexican mainland, one of my first stops was Zacatecas. It is a so-called silver city and the largest town in the state of that name. Starting in the mid-sixteenth century, Zacatecas's mines produced vast amounts of the precious metal and made many, in addition to the Spanish crown, very rich. Its economic importance and the magnificence and exquisite preservation of its historic center have earned it a place on the list of World Heritage Sites.

Zacatecas is tremendously prosperous to this day, with hip, modern cafés and restaurants and spectacular museums. Two of its newest museums are good examples of not just its wealth but its sophistication and awareness of the world. Museo Pedro Coronel is housed in a seventeenth-century Jesuit building and is named for its patron, an artist and native of Zacatecas. It has a magnificent assemblage of art from around the world, including works by Picasso, Dalí, Chagall, and other European Modernists. Pedro's brother, Rafael, also a painter, has endowed another fine collection. Housed in a seventeenth-century convent, Museo Rafael Coronel boasts thousands of indigenous Mexican masks he donated. Rafael's father-in-law was the celebrated Mexican painter Diego Rivera, whose work is also represented here.

The major place of worship, the Catedral de Zacatecas, is a masterpiece of the Mexican Baroque's ultra-elaborate Churrigueresque style, with vast amounts of sculptural ornamentation styled after the work of the late seventeenth-century Spanish architect and sculptor José Benito de Churriguera. Built in the early 1800s, the cathedral is situated on a narrow street. Like other major structures in town—churches, theaters, civic buildings, residences, schools, and more—it feels to me as though it's been injected into the little lanes of the Indian village that preceded the Spanish city historically. The wildly embellished façade looming overhead and stretching to the heavens enhances the sensation of the cathedral being a visitor from a distant place.

Zacatecas

In Catholic Church architecture, openings are important, especially the front door, which welcomes congregants to the beginning of their journey of faith. The main doorway of the Catedral de Zacatecas does so with great flamboyance—even more so at night, when lights exaggerate the intricacy of the façade. It's an invitation to enter the temple that can't be missed. In Catholic churches, statues of saints and other decorative elements were originally intended to convey this message to those who could not read. Meanwhile, the religious and the political were inevitably entwined, with heraldic insignia identifying a church's patrons and the religious order that built it. Though the Catedral de Zacatecas's other doorways and windows are also decorated, much of the remaining exterior surface is—as is also typical of Catholic churches—plain stone blocks.

83
The west elevation of the Baroque Catedral de Zacatecas.

83

84
A façade of the street called Callejón de Gómez Farías.

85
Dancing from plaza to plaza and bar to bar to the infectious local music, *tamborazo zacetecano.*

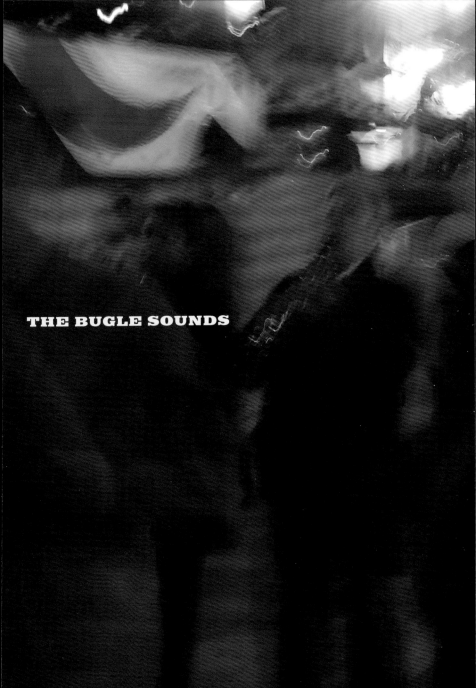

THE BUGLE SOUNDS

85 (previous page)
Dancing from plaza to plaza and bar
to bar to the infectious local music,
tamborazo zacetecano.

One of the marvelous experiences of Zacatecas is hearing the local musical specialty, tamborazo zacatecano. Many of us are familiar with mariachi music, but this is another style entirely. Tamborazo groups are small brass bands, typically trumpets, trombones, saxophones, and a bass drum, though there are regional variants. They are descended from military bands imported to Mexico in the 1860s by the nation's Habsburg ruler, Maximilian I. The wind-band, or banda, tradition was subsequently taken over and popularized by insurgents during the Mexican Revolution.

One of the most famous tamborazo zacatecano compositions is Genaro Codina's "La Marcha de Zacatecas," or The March of Zacatecas. Reminiscent of works by John Philip Sousa, the song is both the anthem of the State of Zacatecas and an unofficial second national anthem of Mexico. Its lyrics are a rousing call to battle: "Oid llamad, suena el clarín / Las armas pronto preparad / Y la victoria disputad" (Hear the call, the bugle sounds / Quickly prepare the weapons / And strive for victory).

My wife and I danced through the streets of Zacatecas to this ebullient music, processing from square to square and passing by amazing examples of Mexican Baroque architecture. People wandered in and out of bars, drinking and dancing, as they followed the musicians. One night, in the zócalo—the public square—next to the cathedral, we watched folkloric skits and ensembles of dancers performing to these tunes, swirling their long, silky full skirts.

The events we witnessed in Zacatecas were more secular in nature than the feast of Nuestra Señora de Guadalupe, which we would participate in when we got to our next stop, Guanajuato. However, the sacred and the secular are never far apart in Mexico. Sanctity suffuses all of life here.

86
A bottle of mescal in the streets of
Zacatecas.

87 (next page)
A folk musician inspires listeners in
Zacatecas.

86

88
Spiral-themed columns climb the
façade of Catedral de Zacetecas.

89
Exterior of Museo Pedro
Coronel, in Zacatecas.

90
The exterior of Igelsia
de Santo Domingo.

90

91
The interior of Iglesia
de Santo Domingo.

92
Steps sweep up to Teatro
Fernando Calderón.

93
The main façade of
Catedral de Zacetecas.

94

Exterior details of Museo
Pedro Coronel.

GUANAJUATO

A. Mercado Hidalgo

B. Underground roads

C. Basilica de Nuestra Señora de Guadalupe

D. Templo de San Diego

E. Jardín de la Unión

F. Templo de la Calzada de Guadalupe

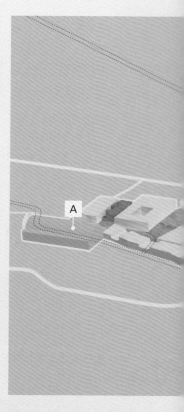

Religious buildings

Public markets

Sequence of public space

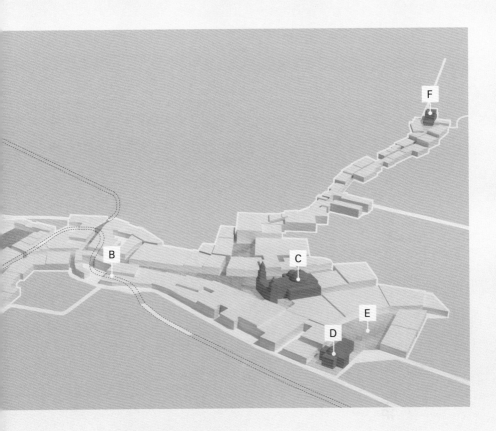

Founded: 1548
Current population: 171,000

Guanajuato started out as a mining city. Its streets
wind through a valley, with narrow alleys that rise and
descend in and around the hilly topography. An underground network of tunnels accommodates vehicles,
leaving the city above largely dominated by pedestrians.

Mercado Hidalgo

200 ft.

Templo de la Calzada de Guadalupe

N

lat 21°01'04" N, long 101°15'24" W

Basilica de Nuestra Señora de Guadalupe

Jardín de la Unión

Templo de San Diego

Guanajuato

Guanajuato is a quintessential pedestrian city, with much to teach about how to accomplish this gracefully. As we seek to make cities in the United States more friendly to walkers, we can think about its solutions. Located in the state of the same name, Guanajuato is another silver city, where vast amounts of the precious metal were mined to support the Spanish Empire. Horrific conditions in the mines here and elsewhere meant the deaths of countless slave laborers and eventually contributed to the outbreak of Mexico's nineteenth-century War of Independence.

After the discovery of silver here in 1548, the town grew quickly on precipitous hillsides. Its tangled network of steeply graded streets and alleyways is mostly impassable for automobiles. However, drivers have an extraordinary alternative. Over the centuries, the river around which the town had been built was directed through tunnels in order to prevent flooding. In the 1960s, the water was diverted yet again, and the tunnels were transformed into a subterranean traffic circulation system.

You can drive into the stone-lined caverns, park there, and climb up stairs to the beautiful city above. The cars are out of the way, walkers can move freely, and the historic character of the town center is preserved. (Yet another option: park on the outskirts of town, and take a taxi in.) Modern designers have been playing with the idea of separating pedestrians and automobile traffic for decades, and here's a city that has already done it amazingly well.

Guanajuato

95

95
Miners in line after a day of work.
Photo: Frank H. Probert/National
Geographic Creative/Corbis.

96

96
Pilgrims walk down a highway outside Guanajuato on the morning of the feast day of Nuestra Señora de Guadalupe.

97

For the feast day of Nuestra Señora de Guadalupe, in Guanajuato, children are dressed as adult members of the Holy Family.

98

In both Guanajuato and San Miguel de Allende, comfort is provided in communal spaces by surrounding plazas with dense, well-pruned Ficus trees. These provide both shade and intimate public spaces. The life of these cities carries on under the bosques.

99
One of many intimate and lively public plazas in Guanajuato.

100
Stairways lead from Guanajuato's underground roads and parking to the town's pedestrian-filled streets.

FRONTIERS

OF THE BAROQUE

101 (previous page)
The Baroque façade of Iglesia de Nuestra Señora de la Salud, in San Miguel de Allende.

102 (opposite)
With its extravagant gold and silver decorations, the Capilla del Rosario, inside Iglesia Santo Domingo de Guzmán in Puebla, represents a pinnacle of the Mexican Baroque.

103 (overleaf)
The elaborate façade of the Catedral de Zacatecas is a masterpiece of the Mexican Baroque's Churrigueresque style.

In my exploration of Mexican architecture, I found it permeated by the Baroque, which had its heyday from the mid-seventeenth to the mid-eighteenth centuries. It is the style of the early stone churches in Baja and the dominant architecture of the country's colonial-era cities, including major government buildings in and around Mexico City's Zócalo.

Baroque buildings feature exuberance, a sense of compelling emotion, and elaborate embellishment that invokes power and wealth. Their decoration appears independent of structure. In Catholic churches, this wasn't just style for its own sake, though. The Church intended the excitement and extravagance to counter the Reformation, which had taken aim at the Church and was siphoning away parishioners to worship more simply in more austere spaces.

The Baroque's path to Mexico started in Italy, moved on to Spain, and thence on to the colony, becoming more exuberant each step of the way. The Society of Jesus, or Jesuit Order, was a key advocate of its ability to communicate. In the tough little churches of Baja, the Jesuits who built them sometimes had the means to add only precious small amounts of decoration. However, even in limited quantities, the decorative flourishes are flamboyant and clearly intended to evoke an emotional response.

Though many of the churches I saw on my travels in Mexico were built on what was then the country's frontier, some of these were constructed in very rich mining cities, such as Zacatecas and Guanajuato. This allowed for lavish decoration involving much precious metal. Complete façades, interior and exterior, were in the most ornate styles imaginable. The cathedrals in Zacatecas and Puebla are excellent examples.

Two other factors help us understand the popularity of the Baroque. Its brilliant colors and lively forms are similar to the aesthetics evident in the arts of indigenous Mexican peoples. The native populations also provided a readily available artistic labor force that was able to immediately adopt this new language of architecture. They understood what was needed, and they could execute it.

104

104
A colorful corner in walker-
friendly Guanajuato.

105
Boys and young men on the roof of a church dedicated to the Virgin of Guadalupe watch pilgrims arrive.

106
The procession arrives at the church.

107
This young Mexican girl is costumed
as Mary for the feast day of Nuestra
Señora de Guadalupe, in Guanajuato.

108
Costumed pilgrims carry gifts and offerings to the Guanajuato church.

SAN MIGUEL DE ALLENDE

A. Iglesia de Nuestra Señora de la Salud

B. Templo de San Francisco

C. Jardín Principal

D. Parroquia de San Miguel Arcángel

Religious buildings

Civic buildings

Sequence of public space

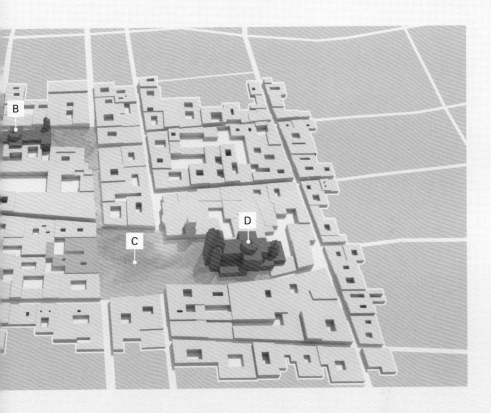

Founded: 1541
Current population: 139,000

San Miguel de Allende was founded after silver was discovered in nearby cities and became an important trading center for the region. It was built largely in accordance with the town-planning and land-ownership rules of Philip II's Laws of the Indies.

Iglesia de Nuestra Señora de la Salud

Templo de San Francisco

100 ft.

N

lat 20°54'51" N, long 100°44'37" W

Parroquia de San Miguel Arcángel

Jardín Principal

San Miguel de Allende

San Miguel de Allende is a quiet little city that has attracted artists and North American expatriates over the years. Foreigners make up about 10 percent of the population of some 139,000 and add a bohemian feel to the traditional ambience. *The New York Times* has called it "Berkeley for retired people."

The city's name is an amalgam of two strains of Mexican history—San Miguel is the patron saint of its first Spanish mission to the indigenous people of the area, while Ignacio Allende was a local man who became a hero of the War of Independence. During the sixteenth century, the original Indian village on the site began developing into a market town and soon became a stopover for people, precious metals, and goods moving between the silver cities and Mexico City.

San Miguel de Allende is about sixty miles from Guanajuato and, like its neighbor to the west, has a central square that is uniquely designed to mitigate the heat of the sun. The Laws of the Indies advised creating arcades around the main plaza. In San Miguel, that is accomplished with a high hedge of cropped Ficus trees that surrounds the plaza, or Jardín Principal. It is a distinctive idea, responding perfectly to the population's needs in this hot climate. The trees create a thick canopy that overhangs both internal and external sidewalks. People gather under them to take advantage of the cool, dark shade.

Towering over the Jardín is the city's main church, the Parroquia de San Miguel Arcángel. Its height makes it visible from afar in this generally one- and two-story city. This was another stipulation in the Laws of the Indies; they decreed that an urban area's major church should be easily visible and, whenever possible, approached by steps, "thus acquiring more authority." The church's fantastically decorated façade is supposedly the work of an untrained but irrepressible native artisan who modeled it after a postcard of a French Gothic cathedral.

San Miguel de Allende

109
Templo de San Francisco, in San Miguel de Allende, is seen in the background, while a simple, bright wall and a well-composed window light up the right foreground.

110
An agave on a garden wall.

LET
THERE
BE
LIGHT

111
San Miguel de Allende stores and restaurants manage without daytime use of electric light.

112 (opposite)
A figure-ground drawing of San Miguel de Allende, shows built and unbuilt spaces, revealing an abundance of courtyards.

113 (overleaf)
Reed shades and plants offer interior spaces subtle decoration, as well as softened light.

Much of the rest of San Miguel de Allende is built around courtyards. The city is said to have ten thousand doors and ten thousand courtyards, though those numbers may well be apocryphal. It is certainly a town with predominantly low structures built around internal spaces. The streets are lined with walls that are painted in rich, warm colors and pierced by stone-framed windows and doorways leading to the inner sanctums.

Because much of the city is so low, these private and public spaces are illuminated by sunlight. The sparkle and quality of light is quite wonderful in the courtyards and in the stylish stores and elegant restaurants that line them. During the day, few businesses in San Miguel need much in the way of artificial light. Clothes and other goods are displayed outdoors, in the natural light of the courtyard.

This experience teaches us much about the use of light. Colors are right and true, and you can appreciate their richness. Fabrics look sumptuous, and food looks fresh from the garden—which it usually is. In contrast, when shopping in a typical North American store or eating in one of our restaurants, you will probably find yourself in an enclosed space lit by artificial light. This alters what you see and, ultimately, the experience you take with you.

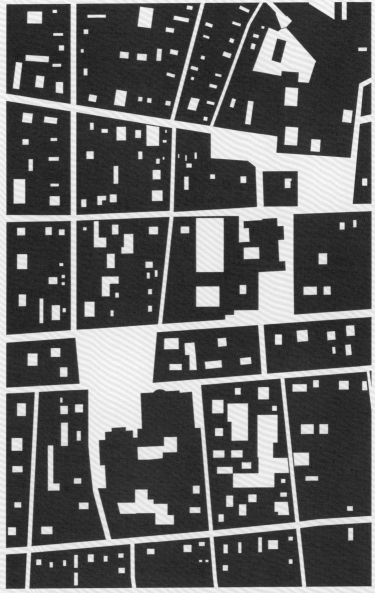

ART AND LIFE

114 (previous page)
Frida Kahlo standing between house and studio, Mexico City, 1933.

115
Frida Kahlo and Diego Rivera, Mexico City, 1933.

Photos: Martin Munkácsi, ©The Estate of Martin Munkácsi, Courtesy Howard Greenberg Gallery, New York, and International Center of Photography.

The spectacular Museo Casa Estudio Diego Rivera y Frida Kahlo was designed by the celebrated Mexican architect Juan O'Gorman for Mexican artists Diego Rivera and Frida Kahlo. The first example of modern architecture in Mexico, the 1931 structure is a good representative of European modernism and was greatly influenced by Le Corbusier.

For me, more than anything else, it is significant because it worked so well for Kahlo and Rivera. In 1934, when they moved in, they were the most important artists in the world. In studios here, they created thousands of pieces. As I walked through the museum, I was thrilled to see the spaces where the art that defined their careers arose.

116
The studio of Diego Rivera.

117 (next page)
The studio of Frida Kahlo.

118
A courtyard in San Miguel de Allende.

118

119
A colorful police station in San Miguel de Allende.

120
Here's what parking looks like
in San Miguel de Allende.

121
This San Miguel de Allende retail establishment, with a beautifully articulated storefront, has apartments above.

HIDDEN

TREASURE

125 (previous page)
The bay and islands at Costa Careyes, in the state of Jalisco, on Mexico's Pacific coast.

126
The casitas at Costa Careyes, in coastal Jalisco, Mexico.

My first trip to Costa Careyes was in the mid-1990s. I was cruising the Mexican coast with my dad, my mom, and my wife, Mary. We were traveling from Mazatlán to Manzanillo aboard the Sumatra, dad's fifty-foot sloop. Our guests were the artist Michael Heizer and his wife, editor Barbara Heizer. Like most of the Mexican Pacific coastline, this area is spectacular, with a lush tropical landscape, small secluded harbors, and occasional resorts.

After mooring in the evenings, we would often get in the launch and visit villages to look for supplies. One evening, we moored off the rugged coastline of Careyes, where we'd heard there was a small hotel. When Michael and I went ashore, we were quite shocked to walk into an elegant beach restaurant where everyone was speaking French. We immediately made reservations and returned with the rest of our party for a wonderful and memorable experience.

127
Surf and islands off Costa Careyes.

128 (next page)
Brilliant colors heat up the shade
at a Costa Careyes pool.

We had stumbled upon Costa Careyes, the ultraexclusive yet low-key resort created by eccentric Italian financier Gian Franco Brignone. It had not only a colorful collection of villas built in a folksy style that emulated a Mexican village, but restaurants and a nearby polo field and stables. During our several-day sojourn, we rested and met the captivating Mr. Brignone, decked out in a serape, as well as his family members.

PRIVATE-HOME
SHORT LIST

129 (previous page)
A double door leads to a courtyard of the home of Luis Barragán, in Mexico City.

130
The street-facing façade of Barragán House.

131 (opposite)
A window and a painting at the top of the stairs near the house's entry.

132 (overleaf)
Watercolor sketches of the Barragán House.

130

There are a few houses that I consider the world's best. They include Soane House, the early nineteenth-century London home of neoclassical architect Sir John Soane. In Pennsylvania, Frank Lloyd Wright's 1935 Fallingwater is famously cantilevered over a waterfall, seemingly suspended in mid-air; while integrated into the landscape, it appears to defy gravity. On a wooded bluff in the Pacific Palisades neighborhood of Los Angeles, Ray and Charles Eames lived in comfortable, functional Eames House, Case Study House #8. Made in 1949 with off-the-shelf materials, it was one of more than twenty houses built in response to an Arts and Architecture magazine challenge. Also in 1949, Philip Johnson's innovative use of materials for his home, the nearly-transparent Glass House, brought the International Style into American residential architecture.

Luis Barragán's own home, in Mexico City, is one of these stellar residences. Built in 1948, Barragán House and Studio has austere exterior walls that enclose light-filled interior spaces, giving it an intimate, introspective ambience. The project was started for a client but soon became the architect's own living space and studio; it is now a World Heritage Site.

In my opinion, what differentiates the Barragán House and Studio from the others on my short list is that it feels as though he designed it in two dimensions. The other houses clearly got their start when their architects visualized a sequence of spaces large and small for a building of one, two, or three stories. In contrast, Barragán's residence seems to have been composed—and beautifully so—elevation by elevation.

It is known that his plans for the site developed over the construction period and that the building functioned as a personal laboratory for the architect. Rooms are different heights. Walls are in contrasting hues. The visitor has the feeling of walking through not a sequence of spaces but a series of compositional studies, one elevation at a time. It is as though you are navigating a work by Josef Albers or Morris Louis. As I walked from room to room, I was in awe of Barragán's choices in color. It was a wonderful reminder of the importance of color and composition in designing a building.

122
A young man paints a monastery
wall in San Miguel de Allende.

OAXACA

A. Zócalo

B. Catedral de Oaxaca

C. Templo de Santo Domingo de Guzmán

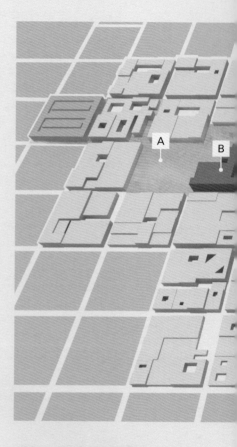

Religious buildings

Public markets

Sequence of public space

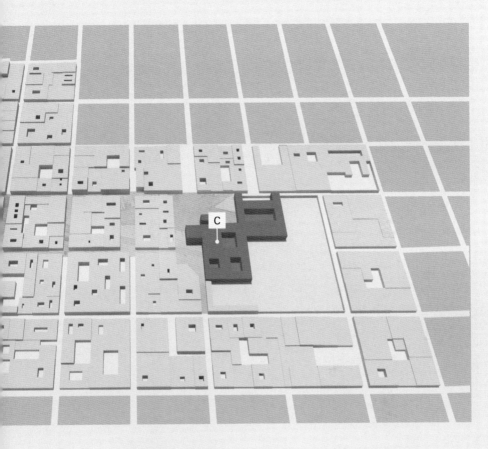

Founded: 1529
Current population: 255,000

When the Spanish arrived in Oaxaca, the area had long been populated, and there were many indigenous villages. Today, in the city the conquerors founded, we can still see a street grid typical of those planned according to the Laws of the Indies.

Templo de Santo Domingo de Guzmán

Catedral de Oaxaca

Zócalo

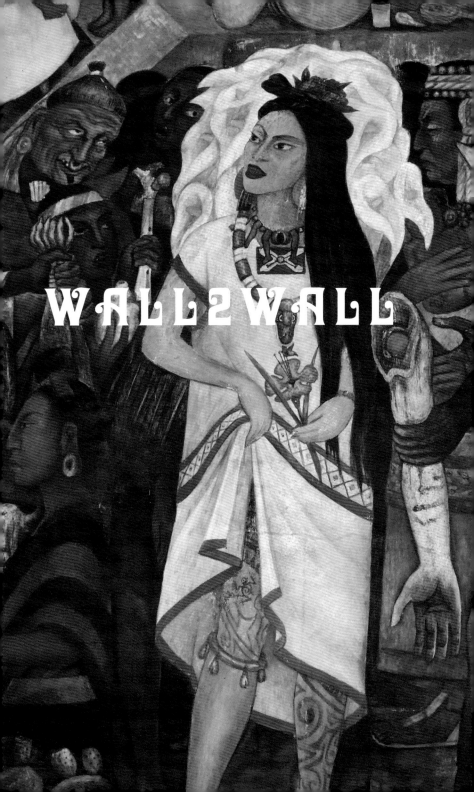

135 (previous page)
Image of a tattooed woman in the Aztec city-state Tenochtitlan, in Diego Rivera's monumental mural *The History of Mexico*. Palacio Nacional, Mexico City.

136
Detail of a mural by Alfredo Zalce, showing Miguel Hidalgo, a leader in the Mexican War of Independence. Palacio de Gobierno, Morelia.

Traveling through Guadalajara, Morelia, and Mexico City, I had the opportunity to see the works of the great Mexican muralists Diego Rivera, José Clemente Orozco, and David Alfaro Siqueiros. The murals I saw were all in government buildings and readily available to the public. A few ideas became immediately apparent. In works of great artistic value, the muralists promoted populist social ideals that presented post-revolutionary Mexico as a mestizo nation of great pride and strength. Indigenous culture and the wrongs suffered by Mexico's native people were prominent. The muralists presented the particular concerns of their day while telling lasting stories of life, death, freedom, and equality.

In the early to mid-twentieth century, when many of the murals were created, Mexico's literacy rate was below 50 percent. As a result, the paintings also functioned to tell the nation's heroic tales to the many who couldn't read and write, just as a Gothic church's religious and heraldic carvings were intended to do for the illiterate Europeans of their day.

137
Detail of a mural by José Clemente
Orozco, showing Miguel Hidalgo.
Palacio de Gobierno, Guadalajara.

138 (next page)
Detail of *Man of Fire* by José
Clemente Orozco. Instituto Cultural
Cabeñas, Guadalajara.

To me, the greatest of the murals is the monumental History of Mexico, painted by Diego Rivera
between 1929 and 1951. The work is in the Palacio
Nacional, just off Mexico City's Zócalo, or main plaza.
It is the most literal and least abstract of the murals
I saw, with vivid storytelling and plenty of graphic
depictions of horrors such as the branding and hang-
ing of Indians. The portrayals of pre-Columbian cities
and city life (including the main market in Moctezuma's capital), of Cortés and the conquest, and of
the subsequent colonial life are simply brilliant.

N

lat 17°04'04" N, long 96°43'12" W

Oaxaca

Oaxaca, in the Central Valley of the eponymous state, is surrounded by a wide variety of indigenous communities that have survived to this day, speaking their own languages and practicing their age-old lifeways. The city itself was founded nearly five centuries ago, in 1529. Its rectilinear plan has perpendicular streets extending from the Zócalo. Throughout the town, the streets themselves are generally narrow and therefore shaded—conforming to Philip II's recommendation for warm climates. In another nod to the Spanish king, the square is presided over by the major architectural representatives of church and state—the Catedral and the Palacio de Gobierno, which was the original town hall.

Historical construction choices, which allow for primarily low, thick-walled buildings, create a harmonious cityscape. Such structures are also practical, since they can resist the area's frequent seismic activity.

The city is replete with magnificent public buildings and residences. In honoring Oaxaca as a World Heritage Site, UNESCO called it "a perfect example of a sixteenth-century colonial town." The continuing vitality of the historic center, with its "economic, political, social, religious and cultural activities that give dynamism to the city," was an important part of winning the designation. The design of the square supports that dynamism. It is a graceful public space that offers lessons for accommodating diverse public needs and activities. Within the square, you will find music, art, sun, shade, food, drink, and places to sit, rest, and meditate—all essential for comfort and enjoyment. It certainly worked for me. One day, I spent a whole morning in the plaza listening to the marimba bands that had set up there. As the music floated through the park and suffused it with a gracious beauty, I felt completely at peace.

Oaxaca

123

I painted this morning view of the Catedral de Oaxaca while seated in the Zócalo. Marimba bands played, families strolled, and the citizens of Oaxaca came out to greet the day.

123

124
A café on the Zócalo in Oaxaca.

133
Streetscape in central Oaxaca.

134
Oaxaca's Templo de Santo Domingo de Guzmán and its associated monastery, now a museum.

139
New Year's Eve in the streets
of Oaxaca.

CITIES OF
THE GODS

The *Millennium Falcon*, bristling with guns and gear, swoops low over dense jungle pierced by crested stone temples. An extraterrestrial soldier waves the starship in for a landing. It's the 1977 release of *Star Wars: Episode IV*, and the ancient Mayan city of Tikal is standing in for a habitable moon orbiting a distant planet.

Inspired by rumors that aliens visited or even built Tikal and other Mesoamerican cities, innumerable authors, scriptwriters, comic-book writers, and video-game developers have featured them as places of mystery and menace. Publicity surrounding the 2012 ending of a five-thousand-year-long Mayan calendrical cycle, and concern that this meant the end of the world, fanned the flames of fear.

Far from being harbingers of doom, these city-planning and architectural masterpieces should serve as inspirations for urban development in the years to come. Marshall McLuhan once commented that we drive into the future with one eye on the rearview mirror. As the journey described in this book took me deep into Meso-america's past and its ancient native cities, I found plenty of lessons for the future.

We live in a time when humankind is increasingly moving into urban areas. During the year of this visit to Mexico, as I was exploring its superb built places, the planet passed a tipping point. In 2007, for the first time in history, Earth's urban population exceeded that of its rural settlements, according to the United Nations

140 (previous page)
I imagine nighttime Teotihuacan.

141
From the top of Tikal's Grand Pyramid, more pyramids can be seen poking up through the jungle.

Population Division. As people continue to flood into the globe's burgeoning cities, the gap will continue to widen. To come to terms with this, we must better understand the nuances of how to build and assemble viable cities. We cannot leave this process to chance. Cities are our future.

In my north-to-south path through the pre-Columbian urban places, I found much that was relevant to this process. I visited Teotihuacan, Monte Albán, and Palenque in Mexico, then crossed the border into Guatemala to see Tikal. All are UNESCO World Heritage Sites. Experiencing them reinforced the idea that urban architecture must include more than the three components that were defined by ancient Roman architect and city planner Vitruvius and that have distinguished architecture ever since. As previously mentioned, these are *firmitas, utilitas,* and *venustas*—solidity, usefulness, and beauty. That is, a work of architecture has long been thought successful if it is sturdy and keeps the elements out, if it has a purpose, and if it is attractive.

There is a fourth component we must also include, and that is the ability of a structure to function as part of an urban composition. This essential principle demands that a building work well within an assemblage of structures that reinforces communal aspirations. In this way, the architecture and its arrangement make places for the ritual, the market, the celebration, the private existence, and the civic life—*communitas*, if you will. This is critical to creating a happy and sustainable future for our world.

The fourth characteristic has been ignored by the Modern movement, which places objects at the pinnacle of discussion. When I was in undergraduate school, I had opportunities during summers to visit European cities and observe their wonderful streets and squares. I saw buildings working together to sustain the practical and spiritual aspects of life. In the fall, I would return to school and to classes with the foremost modernist architects of the day. When other students and I raved about what we had seen abroad, our professors would say, "Forget it. That's the past. We don't care."

Those great architects drummed into us the idea that individual buildings were what was important, not combinations of them. They were comfortable with the cold, severe buildings they designed. They didn't want the public thronging into and around the structures. As a result, their legacy was beautiful buildings but not workable cities.

In cities around the world, I have observed that the most glamorous buildings may be rejected by the people who are supposed to be using them. Often, they simply aren't at ease in these challenging spaces. Such buildings often sit alone on their streets or in their green spaces—haughty beauties that don't acknowledge the structures around them or the human community. It is long past time to rethink the modernist notions of what makes a successful building.

Creating a place has always been a statement of power. Augustus Caesar's Rome and the plans for Washington, DC; Rockefeller Plaza; and innumerable civic, religious, private, and corporate projects around the world have been a way for those in charge to declare themselves. Today, that power increasingly and appropriately rests in communities' determination to create the structures they need. Of course, for large-scale undertakings, some kind of centralized planning and execution will always be needed.

What first struck me about the pre-Columbian cities I visited was the magnificence of their compositions. At each site, the inhabitants, marshaled by their rulers, had made a tremendous investment of time and resources in architecture. They had produced many splendid structures and had arranged them so that they worked together to support human society. To me, these achievements underscored yet again the fact that caring for community is essential to the well-being of the planet's quickly urbanizing population.

The Mesoamerican cities have such a strong sense of unity that they appear as single monumental sculptures. As I explored them, I felt that those who executed them over the centuries held fast to the original intention, even as they added to, modified, and replaced various elements. One obvious overarching principle in each was a devotion to the life of the spirit. Worship was woven into every aspect of the architecture, its arrangement and its decoration, and thereby into the inhabitants' lives. At Teotihuacan, heaven and earth come together in the Pyramid of the Sun, a giant temple mount built over a tunnel ending in a series of chambers below the center of the pyramid. Iconography such as the Feathered Serpent evokes a concordance of earth and sky.

Since human beings have been gathering together in cities, there are two main ways they have organized them: along a street or around plazas. The ceremonial center of one site I visited, Teotihuacan, was arranged around a grand boulevard. Its secondary areas, including residential compounds, were around squares. At Monte Albán, there were no boulevards. Its rulers created a sense of order and control by placing the most important structures around a massive plaza that dominated the whole. They enhanced this impression by siting the

142

majestic surrounding buildings so they appeared more symmetrically arranged than they really were. Palenque and Tikal also had a plaza-style organization, with paths linking one large and multiple smaller squares.

To reanimate the cities and discover what they tell us about creating our own admirable urban places, I imagined them as living places. Like many before me, I reflected on what they would have been like with inhabitants filling them. I visualized nobles, peasants, merchants, and officials strolling the sweep of Teotihuacan's central boulevard, the mile-and-a-half-long Avenue of the Dead. I saw shoppers haggling with farmers and artisans, priests processing, children playing, and soldiers striding along. I thought about people walking down paths and passageways, crossing plazas, and passing by fountains and art objects.

I imagined the inhabitants entering and exiting the range of institutions that made up the city. Here, as in other ancient cities, there were public places—temples, government buildings, markets, ball courts, military barracks, prisons, and burial places—and private ones, including elite and ordinary habitations. Open space included communal plazas and private courtyards. Aqueducts and other forms of irrigation supported farms and garden plots. The inhabitants would have been varied as well, with original peoples, later incomers, and temporary residents. Some of the population numbers were large—in the tens of thousands, and perhaps as many as two hundred thousand at Teotihuacan.

Each ancient city was like a functioning organism in its day, with all parts working together to move it forward. This is despite what must have been a lively mix of people, an incredible range of structures, varying terracing and terrain, and many unique sequences of spaces. The architectural success of each city is due in large part to a cohesive town plan, a consistent building style, and the use of similar materials throughout. Though they are bare stone today, in their time they were largely covered with stucco—made by burning limestone and mixing it with sand and gravel—and painted. This would have had the effect of both relating them visually one to another and making them stand out from their surroundings. Their harmoniousness reminded me of Italian hill towns, which have an array of dissimilar structures while presenting a unified appearance. As we make the cities of the future, the elements at our disposal will not have uniformity of this sort and on this scale. Our challenge will be to achieve unity and workability via diversity.

In sketching and making watercolors of the pre-Columbian cities, I was aware once more that I find these media valuable for what they do not tell us, as well as for the information they do impart. To paraphrase McLuhan again, the medium is an integral part of the message. As artists work, they decide to include and emphasize some aspects of a scene while ignoring or eliminating others. In the old cities, I found myself continually deciding what mattered to me and what I wished to convey about their messages for our future.

143

These four diagrams—of Teotihuacan, Monte Albán, Palenque, and Tikal—depict universal forms of urban organization. Teotihuacan, dated to approximately AD 400, is organized along a grand avenue. Monte Albán, approximately AD 600, is organized as a rectangular plaza. The city plan, in fact, is the plaza. The structure in the middle is actually a rock outcropping carved into a building. Palenque and Tikal, approximately AD 700, are not only similar in chronology but also in architectural style and organization. Both sites comprise a series of paths and causeways that link grand plazas with other squares.

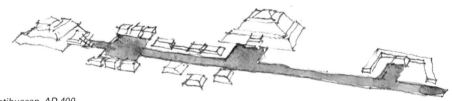

Teotihuacan, AD 400

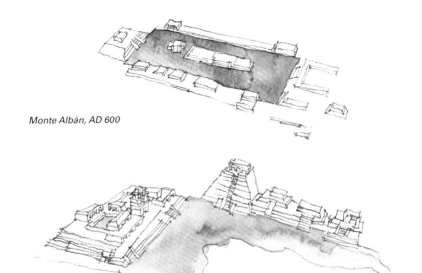

Monte Albán, AD 600

Palenque, AD 700

Tikal, AD 700

TEOTIHUACAN

A. Pyramid of the Moon

B. Plaza

C. Pyramid of the Sun

D. Avenue of the Dead

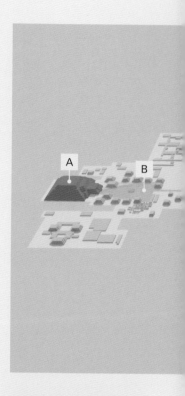

Religious buildings

Sequence of public space

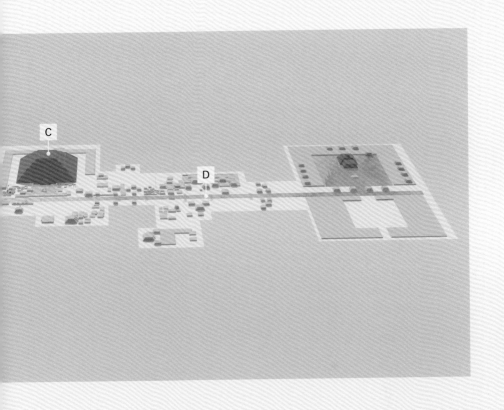

Pyramid of the Moon

Plaza

Pyramid of the Sun

Avenue of the Dead

N

lat 19°41'33" N, long 98°50'37.68" W

Teotithuacan

500 ft.

The first of the pre-Columbian cities I visited was Teotihuacan, about thirty miles northeast of what is now Mexico City. Built during the first several centuries AD, the site's huge stepped temples and pyramids were meticulously aligned to the movements of the sun and other heavenly bodies. This imposing architectural and artistic achievement, set in a broad highland plain, bespeaks a sophisticated knowledge of cosmic events and a profound understanding of the organization of the universe.

In its heyday, Teotihuacan was the largest city in the Americas and one of the largest in the world. Throughout its extended landscape and long lifetime as a metropolis, it supported a multitribal population of at least one hundred thousand souls—some scholars say as many as two hundred thousand. That is yet another achievement, since providing a large population with food and water for centuries bespeaks excellent planning and use of resources.

In archaeologist George L. Cowgill's wise and eminently readable review of research on the city, *Ancient Teotihuacan: Early Urbanism in Central Mexico*, he makes a case for seeking out the lessons of such urban places. With research, he writes, "we develop an idea of what worked and what didn't and thereby improve present-day planning efforts." To have lasted as long as the Teotihuacan polity did, he writes, "Teotihuacanos must have been doing something right."

The grand ceremonial center is only about one-tenth of what was the entire urban area. The heart of the city is defined by the mile-and-a-half Avenue of the Dead, overlooked by the massive Pyramids of the Sun and Moon and rimmed by temples, courtyards, market plazas, residences, administrative offices, and military barracks. The assemblage is a perfect example of the city as a reflection of the cosmos—a community that takes care of its inhabitants' earthly needs and heavenly aspirations.

After a mysterious and catastrophic fire in around AD 600, Teotihuacan disintegrated as a functioning city.

Teotihuacan

However, it remained influential, as successor civilizations imitated its architecture and iconography. Sixteenth-century Spanish chronicler and Franciscan priest Bernardino de Sahagún reported that the Aztecs of that time traveled there to make offerings, collect artifacts, and bury their dead rulers. The name the Aztecs gave the city—variously translated as "the place where men became gods" or "the place where the gods were born"—reflects this strategy of legitimizing themselves through a connection to it.

Centuries later, it is still a pilgrimage destination. Teotihuacan and the other pre-Columbian cities I visited were filled with Mexican tourists. This is their heritage, and they seek out its meaning to this day. On the spring equinox, as many as one million people visit to climb the pyramids at Teotihuacan and open their arms to the rising sun.

144
This fantasy watercolor imagines Teotihuacan's Pyramid of the Moon overlooking a lively plaza.

145

In 1967, I took this photograph of the Pyramid of the Moon just as a ray of sunshine struck it.

146
Partaking in their heritage,
Mexican tourists climb the
Pyramid of the Sun.

147
Visitors, mostly Mexican, promenade along the Avenue of the Dead. The Pyramid of the Moon is in the background.

148
Detail of the wall construction of a
Teotihuacan residential compound.

149
This detail of Teotihuacan's Temple of Quetzalcoatl, the Feathered Serpent, is now at the National Museum of Anthropology, Mexico City.

150
A statue of water goddess Chalchiuhtli-cue, once in front of the Pyramid of the Moon, is now at the National Museum of Anthropology.

150

151
A sculptural work from Teotihuacan that has found its way to the National Museum of Anthropology.

152
Terraced stone structures
define the plaza and front
the Pyramid of the Moon.

MONTE ALBÁN

A. Sunken Courtyard

B. Ballcourt

C. Observatory

D. Plaza

E. South Platform

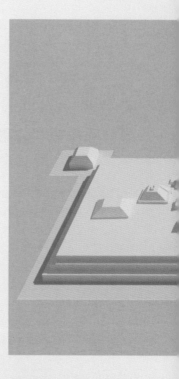

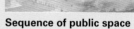

Religious buildings

Sequence of public space

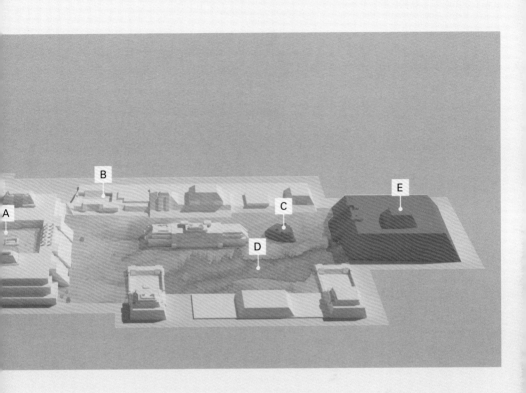

Sunken Courtyard

Ballcourt

Plaza

Observatory

South Platform

N

lat 17°2′38″ N, long 96°46′4″ W

Monte Albán

200 ft.

This ceremonial site, near the present-day city of Oaxaca and about three hundred miles southeast of Mexico City, was carved into the top of a mountain. Monte Albán, or "White Mountain," was inhabited for thirteen centuries, beginning in about 500 BC. It was the center of Zapotec life for much of that time, with a population in the tens of thousands. Its architects began the site we see today with a massive public-works project. Starting during approximately the first century BC, they leveled the top of the mountain and paved it, all without modern earth-moving equipment or tools.

They subsequently built great pyramids and extensive open areas. The civic plan mirrors the contrast of the holy mountain with the vast surrounding plain. The central Great Plaza is a majestic sweep that measures about nine hundred by six hundred feet. Because of its north–south axis, doorways of its temples face both rising and setting sun. Both from a distance and within its bounds, the city is a glorious and overwhelming sight.

Set about fifteen hundred feet above the plain, Monte Albán was probably easily defensible, as the inhabitants would have been able to see anyone approaching down the valleys that come together at its base. The populace was not only in a defensive posture, though. At the apex of its influence, Monte Albán controlled much of the Valley of Oaxaca. A set of carved stone slabs depicts the mutilated remains of enemy soldiers.

The city's distance above the valley floor also placed its ceremonial center closer to the heavens. An early name for the site—Jaguar Mountain—offers a clue to that connection. The designation evokes the power and beauty of one of the Americas' largest land predators. As creatures that were both feared and respected, jaguars were avatars of the gods and an emblem only the strongest could assume.

Baked-clay and stone models of temples have been unearthed at Monte Albán, archaeologist Joyce Marcus writes in *The Art of Urbanism: How Mesoamerican*

Monte Albán

Kingdoms Represented Themselves in Architecture and Imagery. They show ephemeral details of construction and decoration that can't always be recovered in an archaeological dig, including long-lost feather and fabric curtains and inscriptions. We can't know how the models were used originally or what they meant to their makers and viewers, Marcus warns. She does, however, speculate that offerings may have been made to them before they were buried.

They are part of a long tradition of miniature architecture, from building and city models to dollhouses and more, that we use to represent our larger built environment. Today I am sitting in a room surrounded by models, including one of the Solomon R. Guggenheim Museum. I readily admit that I admire—even idolize—them, and the ancients may have felt the same way about their model buildings.

153 Structures on Monte Albán's North Platform.

154
A view from Monte Albán's North Platform toward the South Platform. A sunken altar can be seen in the plaza, and a ballcourt is to the left.

155
This platform is on the west side of Monte Albán's plaza. Glyphs are seen in the foreground.

156

At first glance, Monte Albán's apparent symmetry overwhelms. Then, studying the layers of vertical organization reveals non-symmetrical aspects, including a celestial observatory that is 30 degrees off axis.

157
I imagine Monte Albán as a living city.

158
From the South Platform, you can see the off-axis observatory in the foreground and the sunken altar at the other end of the plaza.

159
Monte Albán's observatory.

Panorama of Monte Albán.

160

PALENQUE

A. Temple of the Inscriptions

B. Palace

C. Temple of the Sun

D. Temple of the Cross

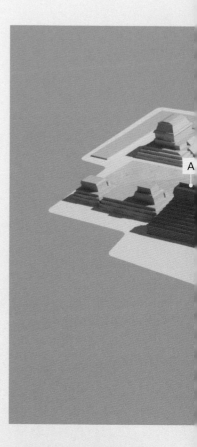

A

Religious buildings

Sequence of public space

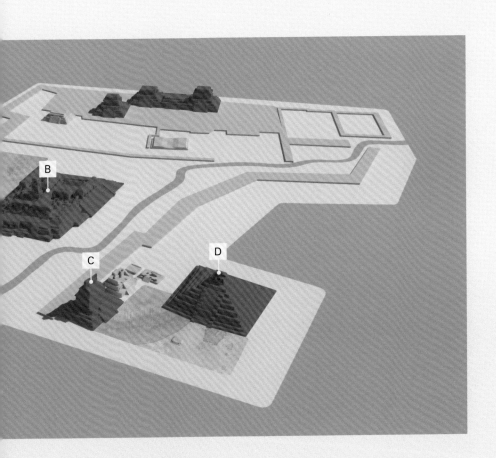

N

200 ft.

Temple of the Inscriptions

Palace

Temple of the Cross

Temple of the Sun

lat 17°29'2.32" N, long 92°2'46.78" W

Palenque

The time-honored notions of what makes a metropolis attractive and livable are apparent at Palenque. I was gratified to find in this Mayan site something I always seek in urban settings—that is, purposeful architecture defining plazas and courtyards, with clear connecting paths leading from one to another. The visitor to Palenque is led through sequences that offer contrasts in experience: progressions of light and dark, large and small, high and low, private and public, landscape and hardscape, civic and spiritual. In Palenque, more than in Teotihuacan or Monte Albán, you can readily see the component parts of a grand-scale urban design and how human beings navigated it.

Throughout the site, I saw openings constructed with the typical Mayan corbeled arch, with courses of stones that each projected over the one below to span the distance from the supporting walls to the center. There is evidence of an elaborate and diversified system of canals, pools, and aqueducts that delivered flowing water to the city.

Settled in about the first century, Palenque was at the height of its influence between approximately AD 500 and 700. It was a successful agricultural and trading center of about twenty thousand that was also continually at war with its neighbors. The ruins, along with the many glyphs found at the site, tell a story of brutal warfare but also of a refined life among the pyramids, with sophisticated courts and an engaging civic life filled with beautiful art and architecture.

One overall organizing characteristic defines Palenque; it is set on a series of stepped-back terraces that the Mayan founders built into the side of a mountain. This arrangement afforded protection against invading armies from competing cities and defined the social hierarchy. The elite kept the top terraces for themselves, and here you see the palace and the largest and most prominent pyramid-shaped temples.

Palenque

HUB OF LIFE

161 (previous page)
A shop in the public market in the city of Morelia.

162
Delicious abundance is on offer in a fruit stall in the Guanajuato public market.

It's been said that you can see all of Mexico in its abundant markets, with their profusion of goods and foodstuffs. Over the years, Mexican cities have come to have two kinds of markets—informal, open-air markets and indoor markets in a government building that rents out stalls to merchants. The former are descendants of ancient gatherings of sellers, which the Spanish sought to restrict to certain areas of their well-planned cities. In this way, they would prevent the chaotic, carnival-like atmosphere that arose when many people came together to buy and sell in the center of town.

In the cities I visited, a walk through the market was a sensory feast, as fragrant cut flowers, pungent chilies, plump white cheeses, baskets of dewy fresh fruits and vegetables, shelves of colorfully dyed cowboy boots, brilliantly painted piñatas, and many more items vied for attention.

The markets aren't just places to shop. Like farmers' markets in the United States, they allow the inhabitants of a city and its surrounding land to meet, exchange ideas and information, and enjoy themselves. They provide the region its cultural and economic glue. Vitruvius wrote about the importance of the emporia for the well-functioning city, while Philip II's Laws of the Indies required the establishment of such places.

163
These boots are made for buyers in San Miguel de Allende's public market.

164 (next page)
Lightweight steel construction helps make Guanajuato's public market a high-volume, light-filled space capable of housing hundreds of stalls.

Scholars say the relationship between town and country seen in Mexico's markets extends back in time to well before the Spanish conquest. Bernal Díaz del Castillo, a soldier who served under Hernán Cortés, chronicled the Spaniards' first sight, in 1519, of the market in Moctezuma's capital, Tenochtitlan, now known as Mexico City. "The moment we arrived in this immense market, we were perfectly astonished at the vast numbers of people, the profusion of merchandise which was there exposed for sale, and at the good police and order that reigned throughout," Díaz wrote. "The grandees who accompanied us drew our attention to the smallest circumstance and gave us full explanation of all we saw. Every species of merchandise had a separate spot for its sale."

Tens of thousands of people came to the Tenochtitlan market daily, attracted by the huge range of goods. Díaz recorded gold and silver wares, jewels, ordinary cotton cloth and elaborate feathered textiles, herbs and vegetables, honey cakes and other cooked delicacies, cacao, salves, tobacco, rope, paper, animal skins, furniture—his list goes on and on. The conquistador finally gave up: "If I had to enumerate everything singly, I should not so easily get to the end."

Sadly, the cornucopia and the intertwining of town and country that Díaz witnessed five centuries ago is now under threat, as supermarkets and big-box stores proliferate. On my trip, I saw them on the outskirts of many Mexican cities. It is not surprising that people flock to them. The big operations can buy in bulk and undercut the prices of the traditional markets' small entrepreneurs. As a result, chain stores have jeopardized the future of some of Mexico's old-time markets, just as they have diminished the vitality of downtown shopping areas in North American cities.

You can't build a pyramid higher than its terminal point. So to increase the height of those at Palenque, its builders topped them with little windowed buildings. The higher you go, the lighter an element must be. Because of the piercings in the walls, the buildings weren't too heavy for the structure below, solving a construction problem and providing ventilation. Combed cornices, or ledge-like decorative moldings around the tops of the buildings, drew the eye upward, increasing the impression of height. Not only was the pyramid taller and more grand than it might have been, it was topped by occupied space. How this space was used appears to be unknown.

After Palenque was abandoned, in about the ninth century, the surrounding jungle closed in, shrouding it from view and protecting it from looters and vandals. Now that it has been uncovered and is visited by hundreds of thousands of tourists annually, the maintenance work is continual, according to UNESCO.

165 This plan view shows that an aqueduct connecting two Palenque plazas provided drinking water and served the palace's indoor plumbing. Beyond these elite areas were irregular spaces for markets and other routine activities.

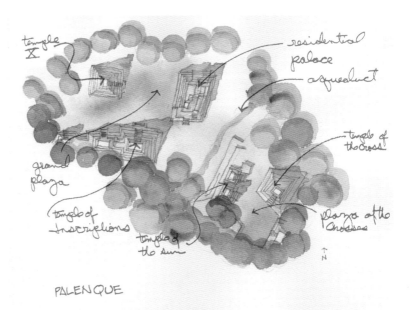

PALENQUE

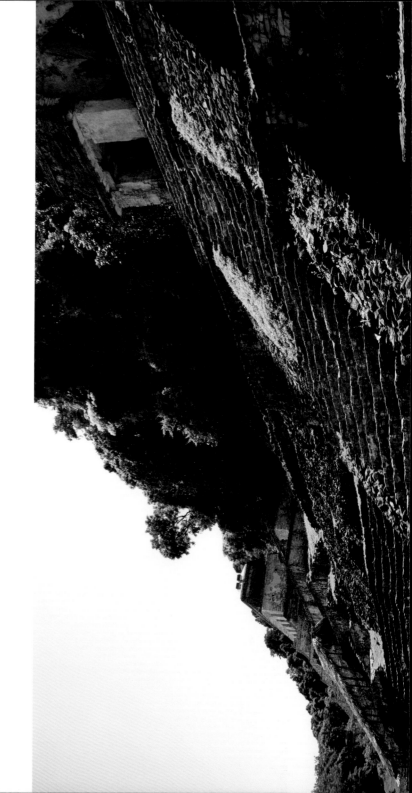

166
Palenque's Temple of the Skull is next to the Tomb of the Red Queen and the Temple of the Inscriptions, on the edge of a plaza.

167
Palenque's palace housed the king, the court, and elite prisoners. There are delightful arched galleries and court-yards, along with a cavernous cellar that represented the underworld.

168
A gallery of triangular Mayan arches along the palace façade. Palenque interiors are mainly galleries or halls formed of arches, and small rooms of corbeled stone.

169
A modern path follows the historic one
that once connected the Plaza of the
Crosses, left foreground, with the Grand
Plaza and palace, with its residential
courtyards and chambers.

170
Surmounting the palace is a
structure called the Observation
Tower, or Prisoners' Tower.

171
A stairway leads to the Temple of the Skull, which shares a platform with the Tomb of the Red Queen and the Temple of the Inscriptions.

172
A carving at Palenque's Templo
XIX depicts eighth-century ruler
U Pakal K'inich.

173
Palenque is a terraced hill town, as seen in this rear view of the Temple of the Sun, which fronts the Plaza of the Crosses.

173

TIKAL

A. Grand Pyramid

B. Temple of the Masks

C. North Acropolis

D. Temple of the Jaguar

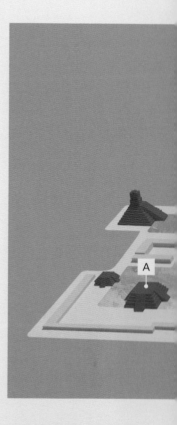

Religious buildings

Sequence of public space

Grand Pyramid

Temple of the Masks

North Acropolis

Temple of the Jaguar

N

lat 17°13'19.54" N, long 89°37'25.01" W

200 ft.

Tikal

This center of Mayan civilization is approached via a narrow road winding through dense jungle. The bus I was riding in proceeded at a crawl to avoid hitting the monkeys, raccoon-like coatamundis, and other animals darting across its path. Brilliantly colored parrots and toucans flitted through the trees.

The bus arrived at a clearing and, through the vegetation, I glimpsed the back of a large pyramid. To get to the front of the structure, I followed a path through one of the city's many residential complexes. The terraced five-story set of apartments surrounded its own courtyard and featured numerous small living chambers that were terraced back one over the other. I climbed to the top of the complex and walked down a narrow path between two chambers.

Suddenly I found myself overlooking the Grand Plaza—a breathtaking view. For occupants of the apartments, this would have been the moment they crossed the boundary between the personal and the communal. It was also a reminder that we all love both protected private spaces and spacious open ones.

And what an open space it was. At each end of the grass-covered expanse was a monumental stepped and inclined pyramid, flanked by additional terraces and pyramidal tombs making up the royal necropolis. Taken all together, it appeared as a vast, interlocking, and fantastical composition.

First settled in about 800 BC, Tikal was occupied until about AD 900. Why its inhabitants left is unknown, though scholars have suggested depletion of resources as a contributing cause. When Tikal was a functioning city, it had a ceremonial center with temples, ceremonial platforms, ball-game courts, palaces, other residences, and large and small squares. Causeways carved out of the jungle link the city center to other, smaller plazas. As I went from one square to another, I saw exotic birds and other creatures, making each journey an adventure.

Instead of being dominated by one massive structure, or a set of related ones, Tikal has a diversity of constructions surrounding the Grand Plaza. Ceremonial

Tikal

activities took place in and around this open area. Military and noble residences fronted it, and market-places were nearby—all very similar to the arrangement proposed by Vitruvius and the Laws of the Indies. At Tikal, it seems that every succeeding king wanted his own residence on the plaza (some thirteen were built) and his own mausoleum.

Tikal was a center of learning, where astronomers calculated movements of the sun, planets, and stars and related them to an intricate calendar. To do this, they relied on the Mayans' sophisticated mathematical system, which was one of the first worldwide to include the concept of zero. Stone carvings and murals with hieroglyphic inscriptions record the city's history and show the cultural interchange that occurred with Teotihuacan and other urban centers of the time.

The central places and activities of Tikal were supported by a much larger agricultural and defense zone. Today the site is still protected by its surroundings. It is within Guatemala's Tikal National Park, which is, in turn, part of the six-million-acre Maya Biosphere Reserve. As a result, Tikal is one of the few World Heritage Sites chosen for both natural and cultural reasons.

174
A plan view shows the connection between Tikal's Grand Plaza and the Mundo Perdido complex.

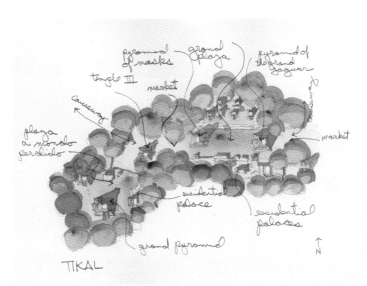

temple on the
Grand Plaza
The Icon of Tikal
700 AD Late Classic
period

175

175
Tikal's Temple of the Masks,
on the Grand Plaza.

176
Builders of the Temple of the Masks
and other Tikal pyramids extended
their height by surmounting them
with rectangular articulations formed
of typical Mayan arches.

176

177
Temples flank the Grand Plaza, a religious and political center. The North Acropolis is at the far edge, and the royal residential complex forms the fourth side.

177

178

178
Another view of Tikal's
Temple of the Masks.

179
The royal residential complex has five levels of externally connected rooms, indicating that much of life took place outdoors.

278
279

180
Along this pathway through royal apartments, holes in the walls indicate where timbers were used as temporary construction supports.

181
A sequence of royal apartments
lies north of Tikal's Grand Plaza.

BACK IN THE CITY OF ANGELS AND ANGLES

Gathering the material for this book was a transformative experience. I grew up in Hispanic-accented California and made many trips to Mexico before the most recent ones. Yet what I saw during my 2007 expedition refreshed and focused my ideas about architecture and the creation of community. In Mexico, I was immersed in a millennia-old culture that had metamorphosed over time while maintaining an exuberance that mystified, enlightened, and energized me. Everything I saw seemed to have happened at a greater scale and with more zest than much of what I had seen elsewhere.

I've always been interested in the development of pedestrian circulation and how it relates to the growth of cities. Growing up in California, I lived in a world of automobiles, where people flowed across long and short distances at a different pace than in places where people primarily walked. My experience would be familiar to most Americans. Whether we live in the country, suburbs, or city, many of us get in the car to go anywhere.

Along the way, I had experiences that suggested other possibilities with a different tempo, including the first architecture I remember visiting. When I was a small child, my parents took me to the V. C. Morris Gift Shop, a San Francisco store designed by Frank Lloyd Wright. We entered the shop through an arched doorway that felt to me, at that young age, like a mouse hole. The entryway signaled an invitation to an unusual space, with a circular interior ringed by a curving ramp one could walk along. The shop is similar to, but far more intimate than, Wright's design for the Samuel R. Guggenheim Museum in New York City. Later, as a teenager, I saw the piazzas of Europe, where the layout also mainly served the walker.

So, from my earliest years, I've been on a quest for ways of crossing space that are different from the usual American way of going about this. In my professional life, I've supported our country's evolution to a new pedestrian experience that serves our changing needs. Old ways of travel are becoming less attractive. In and around many of our cities nowadays, the roadways are gorged with automobiles, driven by dangerously distracted drivers. Even in the rural west, ribbons of black-top that once stretched, empty, to the horizon are now crowded highways. For traveling longer distances than one can comfortably walk, access to convenient, safe public transportation is essential. It looks as though the widespread use of robotic cars is also a real possibility, so road travel may one day be like taking an elevator.

Meanwhile, pedestrian outings are becoming richer, with the potential for beautiful and intriguing encounters as walkers move through sequences of spaces. In the trips to Mexico described in this book, I encountered this abundance at every turn and at what I think of as three different scales. At the small end of the scale, the churches I visited epitomize this ideal within one building. As you have read in "Baja and Beyond" and "A Rosary of Cities and Spaces," the visitor transits a sequence of spaces. In the churches, this passage supports the religious experience. At a larger and more complex scale, the hamlets, towns, and cities that grew up around the churches provide an array of facilities that the inhabitant or visitor moves among. There is always a plaza, and there may be several, as well as places to live, work, govern, grow and sell food, make and sell other products, and so on. At the epic end of this scale are the pre-Columbian cities, with their gigantic temples.

In my professional life, I have operated at these three scales, designing small buildings such as churches, whole communities, and monumental buildings such as skyscrapers. Design ideas I observed in Baja churches guided me as I created new sacred spaces. The lessons of the old churches apply broadly to designing sacred spaces of many faiths. The eighteenth-century build-ers faced many of the challenges we cope with today, and even an abstract modern design can employ their techniques.

In creating an environment for worship, the architecture must support the intended rituals. One fundamental task for the designer is planning a structure that orchestrates the congregation's passage from the material world to the spiritual realm. This path, once defined, prepares worshipers for what they are about to experience. The task may be accomplished in many ways. To begin with, if the building looks like nothing else in its environs, and is perhaps bigger or taller or made of different materials from those of surrounding structures, the viewer immediately picks it out and notices it from afar. Certainly for native converts in Baja and mainland Mexico, the early churches must have offered an invitation to a place and an experience they could never have imagined.

In addition to appearing special, a sacred building must take its visitors through a meaningful architectural sequence. They arrive; they perceive certain symbols or significant ornamentation; they pass through several spaces that lead them to the sanctuary. They feel part of a spiritual gathering. As in most Catholic churches, one of the first interior experiences in the Jesuit mission churches is of the baptistery, which tells visitors that baptism is the beginning of this religious journey. As they move further into a Baja church, the temperature changes; it is cool and a respite from the ferocious desert heat.

The challenge has been using the time-honored approaches to support contemporary spiritual requirements and rituals. My chapel for Chapman University's Fish Interfaith Center, in Orange, California, needed to support multiple religions. Throughout the building, artworks include commonly held elemental imagery— of light, water, sky, life, and death—to accommodate this. The approach to the building takes visitors past a lantern-like tower and under the cool shade of a pergola, from which they see unusual plantings and pavement markings that evoke a musical score. The fragrance of blooming flowers wafts by. They enter the chapel through a sculpted steel-and-glass door that opens

Lady Queen of Angels Catholic Church, in Newport Beach, California. Photos: Joe Aker for AC Martin, Tim Griffith for AC Martin, and Art Gray for AC Martin.

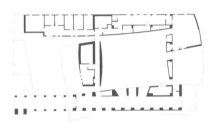

182

The needs of today's worshipers are accommodated in, from top, the Padre Serra Parish Church, in Camarillo, California; Chapman University's Fish Interfaith Center, in Orange, California; and Our

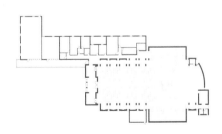

onto a long corridor, at the end of which is an artwork evoking the sun. All of this readies them to enter the high-ceilinged, light-filled sanctuary.

Similarly, in the Padre Serra Parish Church, in Camarillo, California, architectural elements lead visitors from the exterior to the sanctuary. On the way, they pass through a series of spaces that are different in volume, one from another. The complex features a courtyard, where weddings and informal gatherings occur. The design also needed to accommodate changes in Catholic liturgy post–Vatican II, including a new focus on the sacredness of coming together. Previously, this had not been a major part of the Catholic religious experience, which had stressed the internal journey. Padre Serra Parish Church's configuration allows congregants to be aware of one another—to look around, to see the community of the faithful. The altar rail, which separates the flock from the priest during the celebration of the Eucharist, is gone, allowing the ritual to take place among the congregation.

Our Lady Queen of Angels Catholic Church is a traditional parish church in Newport Beach, California. Among other elements, it uses very high windows, like those of the Baja churches, to train daylight onto the altar and focus the attention there. In this structure, the sequence of spaces and the distinctive play of reflected light combine to reinforce a sense of ritual.

183 The Wilshire Grand Plaza will be a contemporary urban plaza, with sun, shade, water features, and places to eat. Photo: AC Martin.

184

184
When completed in 2017, the Wilshire Grand Center, commissioned by Korean Air, will redefine the Los Angeles skyline with an airline wing profile. Photo: AC Martin.

As I stand on a high floor of the Wilshire Grand Center in downtown Los Angeles, a structure that I designed from 2013 to 2015, I can see my work on a larger scale. The skyscrapers and plazas I have created surround me, along with those of my family's century-old firm, AC Martin—from the ziggurat-shaped tower of City Hall, which my grandfather collaborated on, to the buildings my father designed after World War II, including the two fifty-story towers of ARCO Plaza (now City National Plaza).

Looking down from my vantage point, I can see even further into the past. The street grid immediately below me was laid out according to the Laws of the Indies, as described in "A Rosary of Cities and Spaces." Philip II's city-planning rules for the growing Spanish Empire were still in use when Los Angeles was laid out in the late 1700s. Based on the ideas of an architect and city planner of ancient Rome, the Laws of the Indies had survived the centuries.

If King Philip could come back and take a look at the epicenter of Los Angeles, he would likely be astonished at the contemporary buildings' designs and materials. He would also see the vibrant city he wanted, with a pedestrian- and enterprise-friendly downtown and prominently placed government buildings and places of worship. As he processed down the streets, with his nobles in tow, the Catholic monarch could even look up and be reassured that many of the buildings point heavenward.

It has taken decades for Los Angeles to find its way back to the intent of the city's original plan from the late 1700s. The Laws of the Indies grid was blurred by the rapid industrial and population growth of the late nineteenth and twentieth centuries and then by a love affair with the automobile. Los Angeles became car oriented, with a downtown that emptied out after the working day, as people fled to its vast and burgeoning suburbia.

The city's dependence on the automobile was exacerbated by the characteristics of its early skyscrapers. As in other American cities, the tall buildings intended, among other things, to glorify the power of the corporations whose names were blazoned across the façade. The buildings' owners and tenants did not want the public to linger around them, so they provided nothing that would encourage anyone to do so. There were no places to sit, take refuge from the hot sun, or share a meal. For years, downtown Los Angeles was not a place where workers or visitors felt comfortable walking around.

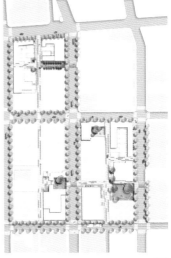

185

This watercolor and plan show aspects of AC Martin's redesign of South Park, to be finished in 2016. The changes will transform this downtown Los Angeles neighborhood, making it pedestrian friendly, with pathways, vistas, and pocket parks. Photo: AC Martin.

Recently Los Angeles has made a concerted effort to reverse this. Among many examples, we at AC Martin redesigned the plaza at 444 South Flower Street in downtown to include seating, drought-tolerant ornamental plants, shade trees, and public art. Now passersby feel welcome to stop and enjoy their surroundings. When they sit in the plaza, they can hear birdsong in the middle of a busy, noisy city. On a recent day, the plantings screened the din from a nearby construction site. Spots to buy food and drink are close by. With such amenities, the city center provides respites, and workers and visitors can feel safe and at ease.

In many countries, cities offer amenities like seating and shade as a matter of tradition, though this hasn't happened in the United States until relatively recently. In my efforts to bring such ideas here, I have been inspired by thinkers like Jane Jacobs. In her 1961 book *The Death and Life of Great American Cities*, Jacobs looked at the mutually supportive interactions, economic and personal, that occur in vital urban areas. She spent a lot of time observing and chronicling these interactions and found that when people know and watch out for one another, everything from the local economy to public safety to happiness is enhanced.

These concepts informed my design for the Hollenbeck Police Station, whose glass exterior supported the Los Angeles Police Department's efforts to present a community-focused police force. Those who work in and live around the station, as well as professional architecture organizations and civic groups, have said that the friendly exterior and light-suffused interior are both beautiful and a vehicle for positive change in the neighborhood.

William H. Whyte's writing, including his 1988 *City: Rediscovering the Center*, also informed my work. Whyte examined human behavior in highly populated places. He found that the city center is "the place for news and gossip, for the creation of ideas, for marketing them and swiping them, for hatching deals, for starting parades...This human congress is the genius of the place, its reason for being, its great marginal edge. This is the engine, the city's true export. Whatever makes this congress easier, more spontaneous, more enjoyable is not at all a frill. It is the heart of the center of the city."

186
The glass-fronted Hollenbeck Police Station exemplifies the Los Angeles Police Department's community policing efforts, beautifies its neighborhood, and provides officers with amenities like restful lighting and desk layouts that support collaboration. Photo: Timothy Hursley for AC Martin.

187

187
People interact and a community forms in the new heart of the University of Southern California, the Ronald Tutor Campus Center, in Los Angeles. Photo: Art Gray for AC Martin.

Speaking of parades, when our firm poured the concrete for the foundation of the Wilshire Grand Center, we invited the University of Southern California marching band to lead a processional to the site. The day was a festive, social occasion marked by fun and interaction—a celebration of the city and its new building. The completed structure will strive to continue providing this kind of experience. It will have a piazza, with tables and chairs for outdoor dining. The building is also sited to provide sun and shade at appropriate times of the day, and it is located across from a Metro Rail station, to facilitate access for those on foot.

By taking the ideal of the pedestrian city to heart, Los Angeles has provided more than pleasant public spaces. The city also has art walks and bicycle tours that attract tens of thousands of participants each month. These activities may be, in an obvious sense, about sightseeing, exercising, or admiring art. However, they are fundamentally social events—about coming together and meeting people in a way that happens only when people move away from the automobile. This is so different from my generation's experience as young people, which typically involved exploring an urban area by cruising along the street with the top down—looking and being looked at, but not necessarily stopping, getting out of the car, and interacting with others.

We haven't entirely turned our backs on the automobile, though. I certainly haven't. The design for a sleek chandelier in the Wilshire Grand Center derives from a computer analysis of an aerial view of Los Angeles's nighttime freeways, with their parallel streaks of red and white vehicle lights: LA's infernal traffic converted into a thing of beauty.

One place in the city where architecture has very successfully provided the social heart is the Ronald Tutor Campus Center at the University of Southern California. When my firm began this project, people studying and working at the half-century-old campus crossed paths in classrooms, cafeterias, and other places. However, there wasn't a comfortable central multiuse location where they could gather. Considering the points made by Jane Jacobs, William Whyte, Christopher Alexander, and other urbanists, and recalling the stellar examples of Mexico's cities, we designed facilities that would make it easy for current and prospective students, faculty, administrators, alumni, and other visitors to meet and interact. Most important, they would become a community.

We know the campus center and its plaza work, because we can watch people using them. So many college courtyards, or "quads," have nearly solid sides that make them claustrophobic, with awkwardly placed openings that are hard to navigate. The pedestrian becomes a prisoner in a box. In contrast, the plaza of the Ronald Tutor Campus Center has "permeable" walls, with sidewalks that enter and pass through the space, making it an easy-to-traverse crossroads. The plaza matches its openness with a sense of enclosure, so people feel sheltered as well. That means they can readily make the choice to linger.

In looking at the Ronald Tutor Campus Center, we can see that today's needs may be met by urban-design theories and town-planning ideas that hark back to sixteenth-century Spain and, before that, to ancient Rome. Halfway around the world and two millennia after the ideas were first promulgated, they still make people happy.

FEEDING THE FLAME

Companions on the Journey: Acknowledgments

As I explored the buildings and cities of Mexico and then returned home to reflect on the glorious places, several people provided critical inspiration and encouragement along the way. Stephanie Woodard, an award- winning journalist, helped express the fruits of my Mexican travels in this narrative. Other important partners were MADWORKSHOP foundation members Edie Cohen and Mary Martin, and staff members Gail Larkin, John Uniak, and Diana Yan, who served as project director for the book. Ricardo Aldape offered perspectives and information. I am also grateful to Michael Hodgson, of Ph.D, A Design Office, who helped develop early ideas for the book.

The process of designing this volume was an extraordinary collaborative journey in itself, taken with Tracey Shiffman and Alex Kohnke. They and their design team at Shiffman&Kohnke brought creativity and structure that opened my mind to exciting new possibilities. I want to acknowledge the work of designer James Ihira and design interns Jonathan Woods, Ely Levy, and Marylouise McGraw. I was also privileged to work with copy editor Sylvia Tidwell, whose encyclopedic mind polished the text.

While I was on the road in Mexico, Martin family members were welcome companions as they took turns joining me on portions of the trip. They saw the splendid sights, danced in the plazas, and held their nerve as we drove along cliffs, crossed rugged deserts, and forded rushing rivers. The family members that joined consist of: my wife, Mary; my children, Lee and Melanie; my siblings, Claire, Mary, and Charlie; and Marilyn Klaus and Stephen Gaboury.

BiblioFile

Here are some of the books that inspired, informed, and delighted me as I worked on this recollection of my most recent trip to Mexico:

David Burckhalter. *Baja California Missions: In the Footsteps of the Padres* (University of Arizona Press, 2013).

William R. Coe. *Tikal: A Handbook of the Ancient Maya Ruins* (University of Pennsylvania, 1967).

George L. Cowgill. *Ancient Teotihuacan: Early Urbanism in Central Mexico.* Case Studies in Early Societies (Cambridge University Press, 2015).

Harry W. Crosby. *Antigua California: Mission and Colony on the Peninsular Frontier, 1697–1768* (University of New Mexico Press, 1994).

Harry W. Crosby. *The Cave Paintings of Baja California: Discovering the Great Murals of an Unknown People* (Sunbelt Publications, 1997).

Bernal Díaz del Castillo. *The Memoirs of the Conquistador Bernal Diaz del Castillo: Written by Himself and Containing a True and Full Account of the Discovery and Conquest of Mexico and New Spain.* Volume 1 of 2, completed in 1568 and translated by John Ingram Lockhart, FRAS (accessed via the Gutenberg Project, 2014).

William W. Dunmire. *Gardens of New Spain: How Mediterranean Plants and Foods Changed America* (University of Texas Press, 2004).

William L. Fash Jr. and Leonardo López Luján, eds. *The Art of Urbanism: How Mesoamerican Kingdoms Represented Themselves in Architecture and Imagery.* Dumbarton Oaks Pre-Columbian Symposia and Colloquia (Dumbarton Oaks Research Library and Collection, 2012).

Felipe [Philip] II [king of Spain]. *Leyes de Indias,* book 4, promulgated in 1573 (accessed via the Gutenberg Project, 2014).

Gloria Fraser Giffords. *Sanctuaries of Earth, Stone, and Light: The Churches of Northern New Spain,1530–1821* (University of Arizona Press, 2007).

Robert H. Jackson. *Missions and the Frontiers of Spanish America: A Comparative Study of the Impact of Environmental, Economic, Political, and Socio-cultural Variations on the Missions of the Rio de la Plata Region and on the Northern Frontier of New Spain* (Pentacle Press, 2005).

Jane Jacobs. *The Death and Life of Great American Cities* (Random House, 1961).

Carlos Jaramilla. *Iglesia del Santo Ángel Custodio de Satevó—Batopilas* (Instituto Nacional de Antropología e Historia, 2003).

Luis-Martín Lozano et al. *Diego Rivera: The Complete Murals* (Taschen, 2008).

John J. Martinez, SJ. *Not Counting the Cost: Jesuit Missionaries in Colonial Mexico—a Story of Struggle, Commitment, and Sacrifice* (Loyola Press, 2001).

Mayo Möller and Edwin Lawrence Barnhart. *Palenque Visto como Nunca Antes / Palenque as Never Seen Before* (Virtual Archaeologic de México SA de CV, 2010).

Andrés Peréz de Ribas. *History of the Triumphs of Our Holy Faith Amongst the Most Barbarous and Fierce Peoples of the New World.* Translated and annotated by Daniel T. Reff et al. (Madrid,1645; University of Arizona Press, 1999).

Joanne Pillsbury, ed. *Past Presented: Archaeological Illustration and the Ancient Americas* (Dumbarton Oaks, 2012).

Jeremy A Sabloff. *The Cities of Ancient Mexico: Reconstructing a Lost World* (Thames and Hudson, 1989).

María Teresa Uriarte. *Pre-Columbian Architecture in Mesoamerica* (Abbeville, 2010).

Edward W. Vernon. *Las Misiones Antiguas: The Spanish Missions of Baja California* (Viejo Press, 2002).

Dave Werschkul. *Saints and Demons in a Desert Wilderness: A History and Guide to Baja California's Spanish Missions* (Xlibris, 2003).

William H. Whyte. *City: Rediscovering the Center* (Anchor/Doubleday, 1988).

ORO
EDITIONS

Publishers of Architecture, Art, and Design
Gordon Goff: Publisher

www.oroeditions.com
info@oroeditions.com

Published by ORO Editions

All watercolors and photographs featured in Joyride are by David C. Martin unless otherwise credited. Diagrams and maps were created by Diana Yan for MADWORKSHOP, unless otherwise credited. The maps incorporate Google Earth aerial images, © 2015 and 2015 © DigitalGlobe. Every attempt has been made to credit photographers and other rights holders and to gain permissions for reproduction. We apologize for any errors or omissions.

Graphic Design: Shiffman&Kohnke
Copyright Editor: Sylvia Tidwell
Text: David C. Martin
Project Coordinator: Kirby Anderson
10 9 8 7 6 5 4 3 2 1 First Edition

Library of Congress data available upon request. World Rights: Available

ISBN: 978-1-939621-73-3

Color Separations and Printing: ORO Group Ltd.
Printed in China.

International Distribution: www.oroeditions.com/distribution

ORO Editions makes a continuous effort to minimize the overall carbon footprint of its publications. As part of this goal, ORO Editions, in association with Global ReLeaf, arranges to plant trees to replace those used in the manufacturing of the paper produced for its books. Global ReLeaf is an international campaign run by American Forests, one of the world's oldest nonprofit conservation organizations. Global ReLeaf is American Forests' education and action program that helps individuals, organizations, agencies, and corporations improve the local and global environment by planting and caring for trees.

... look off ... Pete returning. About ½ ho...
... returning but a group of men
on way. We were ...
America woman had requested help and
negotiate a price and got TC to ...
Several failed attempt the ...
looked was the ... riding with a
... about 5 men ...
thru the town. We made ...
way now ... to ... Sam Farmer. We ...